AWAKE
TO
LOVE

IRIS SPARKES

Published by

MELROSE BOOKS

An Imprint of Melrose Press Limited
St Thomas Place, Ely
Cambridgeshire
CB7 4GG, UK
www.melrosebooks.co.uk

FIRST EDITION

Cover designed by Melrose books

ISBN 978-1-909757-35-6

Printed and bound in Great Britain by:
CPI Group (UK) Ltd, Croydon, CR0 4YY

FSC
www.fsc.org
MIX
Paper from
responsible sources
FSC® C013604

DEDICATION

For the wonderful gift of life.

ACKNOWLEDGEMENTS

Grateful thanks to my daughter, Gillian, for all her valuable support in so many ways and on her choice of images that so enhance the words.

Also, thank you again, to all the team at Melrose for the important role of bringing everything to fruition.

CHAPTER 1

The Angel that presided o'er my birth
Said little creature formed of Joy and Mirth
Go love without the help of anything on Earth

William Blake, poet

Perhaps it's my astrological connection to the planet Venus associated with the Earthy sign of Taurus that has given me a deep appreciation of the beauty that surrounds us in our everyday lives. Shapes, colours, sounds, the musical quality of words…

In a childhood without television, my fanciful imagination was caught by a fairy tale picture, or a few poetical lines on picture postcards sent to my sister and I. What little treasures.

"Windy, beautiful and fine is the air
Right up here, among the pines, everywhere"

Fortunately, there were the musical evenings. A regular event. We brought out the teacups, cakes and music scores. Friends and family would sing well-loved tunes around the piano, played by my aunt: a special moment of music and good humour. My favourite illustrated song book depicted the A.A. Milne characters.

"Half way up the stairs is a stair where I sit
There isn't any other stair quite like it
It's not at the bottom; it's not at the top
But this is the stair where I always stop"

And, of course, there were Sundays. The mysterious High Church ritual in the rather dark atmosphere of St Albans. The candle bearers moving backwards and forwards across the sanctuary. A bell ringing out at special parts of the service and the boat-boy, a small child who carried incense for the server who wafted it out into the congregation, a large one at that time! On feast days such as Easter, I proudly watched the choir processing around the church singing hymns like "Hail thee, festival day". My father was one of the soloists.

The rest of the time the adult world seemed so dull around me.

School days were pretty cheerless. In senior school, English lessons introduced us to Shakespeare's delightful, magical world in *A Midsummer Night's Dream*. We acted it out in a dreary school room. Would it have been such a stretch of imagination to have taken us to a nearby park or wooded area? We also spent many hours studying the rather boring village life of *Cranford* by Mrs Gaskell. It was much more exciting when we were taken to see the film *Henry V* although it can't be compared to "Harry Potter" that grabs the imagination of our youngsters today.

As for my musical education, I can recall sitting in a rather hallowed front room: never warm in winter, beside a miserable looking piano teacher who emphasised the learning of scales. How I ever retained a love of music I don't know! In later years, a Welsh lady encouraged us to play what we wanted and I had no hesitation in choosing pieces by the French composer Claude Debussy. I also always liked to play hymn tunes with their lovely harmonies, so much so that for my 17th birthday my mother and father bought me a "Songs of Praise" hymn book which I still have!

Schooldays came to an end after a rather unhappy puberty. I wanted to stay like Peter Pan in Never, Never Land, and not grow up into the dreary adult world I saw around me. Thankfully, the boyfriends that seemed to appear in my life did much to help bridge the gap throughout this difficult time.

CHAPTER 2

Things just happen in the right way, at the right time.
At least they do when you let them

The Tao of Pooh Benjamin Hoff

I left school with no academic achievements, very little self esteem, and obtained a job as a machine operator in the accounts department of the local waterworks company.

The secretary of the company was also the local impresario who put on musical events in the local cinema. When he discovered my own interest in music, he asked me if I would like to organise the programme selling at these events. Of course I would!

How exciting it was to join the after concert gatherings, to rub shoulders with many of the well known performers of the time. My cultured cavalier extended invitations to London musical events. Thus was the memorable first, and to date only, visit to Covent Garden to see *Der Rosenkavalier (Knight of the Rose)*. I was fascinated by the atmosphere of an opera house, the orchestra, the singers, the scenario with its romantic theme and the tension surrounding the different relationships. Looking back, I'm sure I might not have been perfectly dressed for such an occasion!

And then there was another charming evening spent at a rare production of a choral drama, *The Immortal Hour* by Rutland Boughton including the song "How Beautiful They Are, the Lordly Ones"

These irresistible opportunities were very special interludes in my life at the time with a charming chaperon who behaved with such courtesy and respect setting meaningful standards for me in later life.

The lamp of life was relit for a while.

CHAPTER 3

The more I discover within me, the greater than me, the more I discover that the greater than me is authentically me

Tensions by H.A. Williams

Looming on the horizon now was a 30-year-long marriage waiting to be played out in the same difficult ways that are so often experienced by many of us.

Being still very young, with a rather Victorian upbringing, I felt I had to accept it all and this approach probably saved me from too much frustration. I never sought to make any fuss or discuss anything very much with anyone, despite much inner unhappiness. Don't explain, don't complain! I was later to learn so much more about the "duality" that exists in our world and what eastern understanding calls Karma, or "unfinished business", being played out from previous lifetimes.

Becoming a full time mother with four children was the comfortable part of it all. It seemed to come so naturally. I never remember being overwhelmed by anything. However, I did take the necessary steps to ensure that four children were where I would stop! Especially when my youngest son was born by an emergency caesarean section operation that saved both of our lives! I came to see everything at this stage as yet another reality for my growth.

My father always had a saying "everything passes", and indeed it does!

When my youngest son was ten years old, I felt I could stretch my wings and see what was going on outside the home. Nowadays, women combine careers and family right from the start, but, like many people of my generation, I had no profession to fall back on and I had just spent the last 20 years as a full-time house mother – so – we start from where we are, the world of children for me.

The Playgroup Association was becoming very active and playgroups were springing up everywhere. The Association being independent and not tied down by the restraints that exist inside the education system, mothers could become Playgroup Helpers and learn, alongside their children, to run groups themselves. As well as the practical experience, excellent courses were developing everywhere. This activity often became a springboard for many of us to launch into all sorts of other openings.

An opportunity came up for me to be begin as a Playgroup Helper locally, which led me on to want to learn more about it all. I was ready to explore the wide world and this, fortunately, coincided with the arrival of my aunt. She had come to live with us in a flat specially built on to the house for her. The house would not be completely empty when the children arrived home from school, so I felt free to start attending a one-day-a-week course at Morley College in London, a first big challenge.

I stayed the distance and completed the course. I was now full of enthusiasm to run my own playgroup, but where was I going to get the money to buy all the equipment? I decided I would try to do temporary work to raise the required funds. This could fit in with family responsibilities. I'll always remember how strange it felt on my first day back in an office after 20 years of being at home!

Everything came together and a few months later I was putting the finishing touches to my first professional project, my own playgroup in the Rugby Club premises situated almost alongside our home. What a thrill it was when the opening day came!

However, destiny intervened and looked down on my work, and probably decided that I shouldn't get out of one routine into another. Barely a year after getting it all up and running smoothly, my husband had news that his job was being relocated… to the north of England!

CHAPTER 4

Open the door for yourself so that you may know what IS
Translation from the *Gnostic Gospels* by Elaine Pagels

We landed in the new area, and another episode was about to unfurl that would have a profound effect on my life.

One of the big advantages in the move was that money went further at this time up north. We chose a large property in which the family could spread out, with an annexe to accommodate my aunt who had come with us. We also had an enormous garden and a field next to the house.

Then we all had to get down to adjusting to life in a country area...

My daughter was now at university and eldest son in 6th form. For us older ones it was an interesting venture, but I completely underestimated the effect it was to have on my two youngest sons. They had been used to a different lifestyle where they strolled down the road to school and with shops, playing fields and friends all within walking distance. Now, in a predominantly rural area, we had to get the car out to go everywhere and the children were transported to and from school by bus. The dialect was very strange to them, too. All this contributed to the eruption of much bigger problems later on.

For the moment, after the initial settling-in period, things were stirring in me to further my interests with the Playgroup Association.

I started having driving lessons before coming up north, and after a few attempts, I finally passed my test, and once I had negotiated the sharing of my husband's car, had enough mobility to accept a Playgroup Leader's position in a local playgroup.

Branch activities of the Association were very active up here, and I was keen to explore a whole range of different perspectives on children through talks and discussion groups. I was fascinated by the books of John Holt: *How Children Learn, How Children Fail* and *Escape from Childhood.* He was an American educator born in the 20s, but way ahead of his time. I also discovered A.S. Neil, another pioneer in alternative education with his famous Summerhill School. I came to realise I would never have had such alternative opportunities had I gone down the traditional academic route. I became so grateful to meet just the right people, for I was appointed the first Area Organiser to look after all the other playgroups in the district. This led me back to the school benches to obtain a Further Education Certificate in Adult Education, which in turn enabled me to tutor playgroup courses in the local Technical College. Later on, an astrology reading revealed that women would play a significant role in launching me.

There was a growing feeling of independence as I was now able to buy myself a small car.

However, heavy clouds were rolling over the home front for my two youngest sons, who had never really settled down: they began to develop health problems. The older one had a lingering bout of glandular fever which interfered with his schooling and his one interest at the time, cross country running. This episode certainly did nothing to help since it came at an awkward adolescent period. Not long after, the younger one developed Crohn's Disease which would lead to two heavy hospital operations over the next 10 years.

I clung to the notion that the earlier full-time mothering they both had might be the glue that would see them through all this. Yet again "everything passes" and indeed has mostly resolved itself for both of them as the years have gone by.

In the midst of all this, I myself was about to have an inner experience that would turn my life completely upside down.

CHAPTER 5

...Not everything has a name. Some things lead us into the realm beyond words...it is like that small mirror in the fairy tales. You glance in it and what you see is not yourself. For an instant you glimpse in it the inaccessible where no horse or magic carpet can take you. And the soul cries out for it...

Solzhenitsyn - Nobel Prize speech

My meaningful childhood religious experiences were tucked away intact, creating an urge towards the intangible side of life. So after settling in up north, I attended various church services which did absolutely nothing for me! Perhaps it was heartening musical communion that was missing. For many years I had loved listening to the Christmas Eve Festival of Nine Lessons and Carols from Kings College, Cambridge. My idea of perfect singing. So, now living near to a cathedral I thought I would explore further over an Easter period and from the outset I was so uplifted by the whole experience, the significance of the Easter symbolism and the choral sound in a beautiful building; so complete and something I had obviously been missing for a long time!

I wanted to be in that atmosphere and went to the cathedral on a regular basis, enjoying the whole milieu. However, like a bolt out of the blue, I suddenly became aware of a very powerful exchange of energy taking place between myself and a particular man. A 'silent communication' developed between us. It was something I had never experienced before, much deeper than just a physical attraction. I knew that it was of great significance, but I could hardly have been prepared for the profound effect it was to have throughout my life, for nothing ever happens by chance.

These words, originally heard at a Queens Hall concert, seem to express my feelings so well…

> *When I am dreaming and the wide world sleeps*
> *Then shall my soul from out this prison flee*
> *Strong and immortal o'er dividing deeps,*
> *When you shall call for me.*
> *Love's sweet communion we will hold apart*
> *E'en though between us mighty oceans roll.*
> *Though tongues be silent, heart shall speak to heart.*
> *And soul respond to soul.*

I've been described in astrological terminology as a "practical mystic", so it was very important at this time to have all my Playgroup Association activities. This aspect of down-to-earth life developed in a very positive way and a few years later, the opportunity came to move on when I took up the position of manager of the local Citizens Advice Bureau. This gave me a grounding lifeline during a period of utter turmoil.

My inner nourishment would come from reading avidly; to explore more and more about the whole meaning of life. Harry Williams, who moved away from the church setting into a community, describes everything so perfectly in his book *True Resurrection*.

> *…This being fully alive in body and mind, it means being a person and being a person is resurrection for all that separates and injures and destroys is being overcome by what unites and heals and creates…*

Over the next 15 years, I continued to soak up all the musical life a cathedral has to offer while absorbing the interconnectedness of everything. A.T. Mann, in his 1993 book *Sacred Architecture* says *"Divine truth is expressed in many forms from architecture to music, from dance to landscape…"*. The discovery of a deeper meaning within brings us closer to our centre and to the sacred. Prince Charles, in his first lovely book *Harmony* seems

9

to recognise this when he says *"in nature's grammar we are often led to acquire some remarkable philosophical insights"*.

During this stage, my steps led me towards the practice of meditation. I encountered a great spiritual master, Guru Raj, and his teachings had a considerable influence on me over the next 5 years before he passed into the higher dimension in 1988. I came to recognise the difference between acquired religious teaching and inner experience of the Truth. I began to feel a need to pull away from certain things that had brought me so much enrichment up until then, as though I needed to have space to assimilate everything.

It was about this time that something that was to be called "The Harmonic Convergence" occurred when the planet would start to awaken and rise vibrationally. I can now see how all these different elements and events were all preparing me for some very special work, some 15 years into the future

CHAPTER 6

As soon as you trust yourself, you will know how to live

Anon

It was timely now to reassess my marriage situation. Astrological information had indicated that I wouldn't be living too close to any family for I had other work to do. Circumstances developed that forced me to make the break from my husband and I began to live alone in 1990. It seemed the only possible answer for me as I now felt certain that there could be no other personal relationship that would ever be satisfactory after such powerful personal experiences with 'the other man' and the link between us would only grow more and more powerful whatever the distance between us.

The separation from my husband was a difficult one. Are there any easy separations?

To start with it meant that my aunt had to move into a retirement home. I myself developed several bouts of cellulitis; inflammation of the tissues in the body. This in itself was probably a blessing in disguise, as it precipitated me away from orthodox medicine for good as I sought solutions through homeopathy. Round about the same time, I learnt that "the other man" had also developed very traumatic health problems, from which he did eventually recover. We are both Taureans and having a strong constitution is obviously a help.

And yet, despite this major upheaval, another new episode was about to unfold; a pleasant one I can now say, for living alone has probably been the most creative time of my life.

The opening event was musical of course!

Following on from an inspiring concert given by a young woman playing the harp in a candlelit castle, I thought that this was just what I would like to do, and, not by chance, there was the opportunity to go to an introductory course. I've been playing and singing with the Celtic harp ever since. I've composed all my accompaniments for many of the well-loved English, Irish and Scottish folksongs, and I've played for quite a few gatherings.

I had been a member of a choir for many years, and despite an ever increasing workload, I always made sure I attended my choral singing practices which were a precious oasis in the busy bustle of the working world.

While still occupied as full-time manager at the Citizens Advice Bureau, I was already exploring new horizons and obtained a diploma in Colour Therapy. This was to be the starting point of my healing work and has continued to play a large, but not exclusive, part. However, to go back to that period, many little events seemed to cross my path indicating the general predominance of colour and sound in my future work

For instance, I went to a gathering where a lady, Dr Norma Milanovich, was introducing us to her book *Sacred Journey to Atlantis* which describes how thirty-four people made a special guided journey to neutralise the negative energies surrounding the fall of Atlantis 10,000 years ago in order to enable our Earth to reawaken. I bought a copy and found she had written a special message in there for me saying I was a descendant from the northern colony of Atlantis, which brought the decoding of the sound systems to birth. Twenty years ago that was lovely to read, but I didn't quite know what it all meant! Nowadays, I have come to realise how intimately sound and colour are linked, a subject I will explore in a later chapter.

Colour again came to the forefront when I was drawn to visit Peru and learnt about Shamanic work and the ancient Inca people. The rainbow is the emblem on the flag of the Inca nation, and still flies above the city of Cusco today.

And, of course, one of the earliest and most intimate signposts indicating my future direction is the token of my first name. Iris, in Greek mythology, was Goddess of the Rainbow: "bright with promise." The Iris fairies bring cleansing, freshness and hope for new starts and better futures. The Iris flower symbolises three qualities: faith, courage and wisdom. In the Iliad, Iris appears as a messenger of the gods, especially of Zeus and Hera and in numerology my name indicates a life path of COMMUNICATION. Yes, I like my name!

And last, but not least, writing has also become a growing interest. I started many years ago in a writers club which was definitely an incentive to discover the pleasure of putting pen to paper in ones own poetry and prose. Since then, the road has gone on and up until *From Caterpillar to Butterfly* was published in 2009, followed by *Over the Rainbow* in 2012.

Living alone has certainly been a most creative period of life!

INTERLUDE

A butterfly, one sunny day, fluttering along his flowery way
Espied a wondrous crimson rose, a fitting place for sweet repose.
With folded wings he made his bed upon the royal petals red,
Whilst on a leaf just overhead, a hairy caterpillar fed.

To him the butterfly addresses a greeting full of interest,
"As you are now, so once was I, ere I became a butterfly.
I crawled around in search of food, hidden in a leafy wood
Until at last my hours were done, and I my silky coffin spun."

"My friend, your talk is too absurd, I can't believe a single word,"
The sceptic caterpillar said, as gravely he raised his head.
When I quit this leafy green, for evermore I leave this scene.
Of whence I came and where I go, not one of us can ever know.
Death is the end and life's bright spark is buried in oblivion dark.

"Not so," the butterfly replied, "for in your language I have died.
And yet I live and so will you. I tell you this is really true.
I once could only slowly crawl, my world a leaf and that was all.
Whilst now I swiftly fly through space and visit many a distant place.
Those leaves I now no longer gnaw, but nectar from the flowers draw."

Dogmatically, the grub replies, "Why tell me such a pack of lies?
Where are *flowers* and *nectar* seen and what does swiftly flying mean?
I know that someday I will die and in the mould my body lie.
No butterfly convinces *me* a butterfly I too will be."
With this conclusion curt and brief, he turned to eat his world, a leaf.

The butterfly, his wings then spread, soon was lost far overhead.
A few weeks passed, the summons came, and in his fat and furry frame,
A premonition strange and dizzy came.
And so forthwith he spun his shroud and in due time emerged
A proud and gorgeous butterfly, who as he flew said,
"Now I know that it's all true!"

Butterfly Wisdom Anon

CHAPTER 7

Oh, world invisible we view thee
Oh, world intangible we touch thee
Oh, world unknowable we know thee
Inapprehensive we clutch thee

In No Strange Land Francis Thompson - Poet

Relationships are ancestral, karmic, coded and complex. It was during this creative phase that I had time to delve deeper into a vast subject that concerns all of us.

Ascended masters, such as St Germain, help to give us light from a higher perspective. He says that all relationships are *"connection within the circumstance and experience with our SELF"*. According to St Germain, "relationship" covers a wide range of human encounters since it can also include how we respond to beauty, for example, in the form of colour, art or music. Obviously, everyone has a very individual and personal experience.

Eckhart Tolle, in his well-known book *The Power of Now* writes *"As you may have noticed, relationships are not here to make you happy or fulfilled... relationship is here to make you conscious."*

Our relationships are intimately caught up with the constant evolvement of all human beings. They are guided by the major influence of how our karma has been played out over many lifetimes. In a ceaseless continuum of cause and effect, we need to have reflected back to us, issues that ought to be addressed within ourselves.

This is a perception that many of us may not have considered, since the theme *"and they lived happily ever after..."* is probably what we all long for! Portrayals in books and on the screen all combine to echo this back to us. Yet it may be more useful to entertain the idea that the particular relationships, past or present, are actually there to further our growth and evolvement. Of course, not all karma is restrictive and relationships are not necessarily burdensome. Many may be very happily fulfilling!

In my first book I devoted a whole chapter on understanding the different sorts of relationships that mankind has been in for thousands of years and which are only now about to change.

Over the centuries much has been written, in many different cultures, about the necessity for contrast as being part of our general evolvement. Myth and legend has often enabled us to perceive the universal aspect of relationships. Mankind has been seen as an inevitable part of the duality that exists everywhere around us; night and day, left and right, and, of course, male and female. We may recall more modern ideas about how "complementary" personalities could make for harmony. It was an ideal that many have accepted as long as human beings have been obliged to comply with universal law.

In more recent times, people have developed lifestyles that are less arduous and therefore more time can be given to consider the whole meaning of life. We are viewing society from new perspectives and this has a direct impact on our relationships. Furthermore, it is not only the quality of our social links that are evolving; it is also the whole organisation. Looking around us we see how the traditional family unit is under pressure. Those who, from the outset, lived "happily ever after" are nowadays a statistical minority. Is it the family form that no longer seems adapted, or individual values that are shifting?

The Muslim poet and mystic Rumi writes *"Because of that fore ordainment every part of the world is paired with its mate...each in love with the other for the sake of perfecting their mutual work".*

In *The Family in Search of a Future*, the author states *"I think a relationship of trust, worth and love between people is the highest and most satisfactory way of experiencing one's humanity. I think it is where spirituality takes place. Without it humans have become shrivelled, destructive and desolate."*

In modern western society, there seems to be an ever growing need to seek personal inner fulfilment. Our expectations are evolving and this has direct consequences on our personal relations, and therefore on their social organisation.

Apart from studies that observe, describe and analyse the evolution of society's behaviour, not much modern literature has surfaced yet on the profound changing nature of relationships. There have been exceptional examples. *The Life Everlasting* published 100 years ago was written by a remarkable woman, Marie Corelli, whom I quoted in my first book. Her work is still considered by many people to be the greatest love story of all time.

> *...And the whole secret of everlasting life and happiness is contained in the full possession and control of the Divine Centre of ourselves, the "radia" or living flame which must be dual in order to be perfect and which, in its completed state is an external force which nothing can destroy and nothing can resist. All nature harmonises with its action and from nature it draws its perpetual sustenance and increasing power...*

Again the Ascended Master St Germain seems to be on the same wavelength when he says in *Twin Souls and Soul Mates* that there has to be complete integration of mind, body and spirit within OURSELVES before we can experience this unity.

These are just a few major indications that when we manage to rise into a higher state of consciousness, we will rather seek to share our wholeness with each other in relationships based on similarities rather than on complementarities.

At this point it seems timely to turn once again towards the spiritual master and teacher, Guru Raj, whose teachings in *The Master Reflects* may help light our path along the road from fragmentation to integration.

CHAPTER 8

Growth is the only evidence of life

Anon

Much has been written about the fundamental subjects underlying human life. There are many veritable masters who probably all give valuable insights. Which one should we choose to listen to? The reply is probably "the one who crosses your path".

Guru Raj crossed my path and his teachings have seemed to cover all the major aspects of my personal questing. I would now like to offer my readers his words and wisdom as a few little guidelines. *(For those who would like to read more these selected teachings are edited by Vidya Andersen Ed. D and Roopa Morosani Ph D and published by the American Meditation Society in 2002.)*

The Master Reflects isn't a book that needs to be read from cover to cover for *"The passages that took on greatest importance seemed to shift from day to day…"*

Guru Raj was a master in the ancient tradition of spiritual unfolding, yet in his early years, he lived in the world earning a living as a businessman in South Africa and raising a family. The last twelve years of his life, he travelled around the world teaching and giving personal instruction in meditation practices.

So, what did Guru Raj have to say?

THE EGO: The ego is the sum total of an individual's personality. In self-forgetfulness, we do not forget the ego. We know that as long as a person is embodied, there will always remain a trace of the ego. But we realise that although I have this ego, I am busy refining it.

SUFFERING: We think that we suffer… we delude ourselves into thinking we suffer. But this is a product of thought and when, through meditation, we go beyond the level of thought, we realise that there is no suffering really. Humankind is not made to suffer.

ATTACHMENT: The cause of all unhappiness and misery in this world is our attachment to name and form. Detachment means you wilfully want to be apart. You become indifferent. Non-attachment is something totally different, it is when you are part of your entire environment, when you partake of everything in your environment, when you can love, and you can become one with another. Individuality ceases entirely. That state is created by non-attachment.

SAMSKARAS: Today we are the product of every thought of the past. Nothing is ever destroyed. All our actions and thoughts are retained within our memory and these are what we call Samskaras. We are nothing but a bundle of Samskaras, of past actions and thoughts that have been heavily impressed upon our psyche. That is why if you keep on thinking negative thoughts, negative thoughts will be attracted to you. If you think positive thoughts, then positive thoughts will come to you. As the inner being the Kingdom of Heaven within is infused into our daily lives the impressions of the past lose their power.

KARMA: The law of cause and effect, or Karmic law, is the principle that as you sow, so shall you reap. The way to improve collective Karma, and thus to improve society, is to improve oneself.

LOVE: Love is the essence of our being. To be able to love truly, to be able to love in totality, you have to find completeness within yourself first, because love is an expression of what one is. Love never judges, it just loves, it just is. When love flowers in our hearts and our souls begin to radiate out to the world, we fulfil our destiny as human beings and the purpose for which this life has been given to us.

SERVICE: All service performed in total humility, because there is sincerity of purpose, will rebound on you tenfold. Everything serves in life. What glory does the flower take in giving its beauty and fragrance to the world? The wind rustles the trees creating its own symphonies. The sun shines, the moon reflects light. Food grows. Such service!

PRACTICALITY: All the philosophies in life are of no value whatsoever if they are not made practical. If philosophy is not made practical it is nothing more than mental gymnastics. It is so simple to be happy, but it is so difficult to be simple.

MIND: The universe is nothing else but mind. Mind is nothing else but matter, existing in various graduations from the totally subtle to the totally gross. People say that they think, but they only think that they think. They do not really think. The slightest experience in the present triggers a memory in the past through the law of association. Expectation is the root cause of suffering.

INTEGRATION: All unhappiness and strife in this world come because people do not function as total human beings. What is lacking is integration of body, mind and spirit.

ENERGY or PRANA: Prana is all-permeating. Prana is omnipresent. That vital force is forever there, was there and will always be there because the manifestation of DIVINITY occurs through the vital force.

ONENESS: There is no adversity in life, there is only opportunity. That which we regard to be adversity might be the very lesson we need to learn.

THE SEEKER and the PATH: To know yourself, you are at liberty to use whatever circumstance is offered to you and learn from it. This is very important. When a person is a true seeker, then the environment that is necessary for their growth comes to them. All circumstances lead them to it.

DIVINE WILL and INDIVIDUAL WILL: You have been given the gift of free will, so do not misuse that gift. You have been given the lamp to light your way home, but do not use the lamp to set the forest afire.

INNER MYSTERIES: Seeking is the purpose of fulfilment. There is a difference between pleasure and joy. Pleasure is momentary, joy is lasting. The light is forever shining. What we are learning to do is to draw back the curtain so that the light can shine into our daily lives.

DIVINITY: The Impersonal God does not create. It just manifests and its first manifestation is the subtlest level of the Universal Mind. This is another name for the personal God. Manifestation is something automatic and spontaneous. The nature of fire is to give heat. We are the nature of God, as heat is the nature of fire.

ILLUSION and MAYA: Remember that with a lump of clay you can make a mouse and with the same clay you can make an elephant. The mouse takes form and the elephant takes form, but what is actual? The clay.

THE HERE AND NOW: If every moment is well lived, then the next moment will take care of itself. To be able to enjoy the moment to its fullest is to enjoy the entirety of creation.

FEAR: Fear only comes from reflection and from memory projecting the past. We fear the future. *What is going to happen to me?* The present is totally forgotten. When you are in the present you are totally fearless. Only memories give you fear.

THE TEACHER and THE TAUGHT: You will find that the teaching of a true spiritual teacher will always be universal. Any principle we set forth can be verified by every religion. We take the essence of truth which is contained within every religion and in every teaching.

EVOLUTION: People do not want to adapt themselves to truth; they want to mould the truth to suit their own needs. That can never be evolutionary. No one can evolve anyone else. One has to evolve oneself.

MEDITATION: The purpose of meditation is to experience the truth.

GRACE: We all know that Grace is an abstract quality. Grace is synonymous with God. There is no difference between God and Grace.

CHAPTER 9

*...You are Pure Energy, with the power of creation, expressing
as a Source of Infinite Wisdom and Unconditional Love.
It means that you are not your body, but the Essence that
surrounds your body and creates it. It means that you are Life
itself, manifesting in a particular way at a particular time
because it pleases you to do so...*

Tomorrow's God by Neale Donald Walsch

In my earlier book, *From Caterpillar to Butterfly,* I explore the important
phases of my healing work that have been a preparation for the amazing
events that are unfolding at this time.

It may be helpful to mention here again, how we have eight glands
that form the endocrine glandular system which regulates the bodies of all
human beings and animals. It was my homeopath in the 90s who suggested
I explore this system and its close association with the chakas (vortices
of energy) which carry our "blue print" for life. I was also helped by a
visit to Peru in 1999 when I discovered the work of the Inca shamans. The
Incas were one of the great ancient civilizations of the Americas and the
builders of Machu Pichu. They practised energy medicine for more than
five thousand years, transmitting the knowledge from one generation to
the next through an oral tradition. I discovered how ancestral bloodline
imprints and our "own agenda" imprints affect the correct functioning of
the glandular system. I followed this up by reading *Shaman Healer Sage*
by Alberto Villodo, a classically trained medical anthropologist, who has
studied shamanic healing techniques for more than thirty years. Furthering
all this knowledge, on a practical level, I rapidly discovered that the

glands of everybody I looked at vibrationally, via dowsing, were indeed unbalanced. I am able to find out information about a person through their name in much the same way one hears the music of a stringed instrument once it is played, for every letter of the alphabet carries a vibration that is transmitted throughout our lives. People often ask if they should give the name they have on their birth certificate, however it is the name we use throughout life that becomes "our tune". One only hears the music of an instrument that is played! Another frequent question concerns the fact that some people have the same names. No problem. Divinity always knows the person I have in my mind!

It was a major breakthrough when I discovered that just by "asking", bloodline imprints could be released not only from the individual person, but throughout their whole ancestral line in a sort of "ripple effect" that also included even the imprints of the non-bloodline parent and their ancestral lines via their offspring.

I am sure that 25 years of practising and teaching very profound meditation techniques that go back more than five thousand years has been the foundation for me being able to tap into the universal healing energy that permeates the universe. I was able to follow up the clearing of my own ancestral bloodline imprints by offering to do the same thing for the meditation students I had at this time. It was very enriching to observe the reactions of one person after another. I was beginning to put together a "healing package" that would grow and grow.

At this time I found "spirit attachment" seemed to be very common, both the human "variety" and the non-human. This could completely shut down the glandular system and even after release, people would require oxygen giving supplements, sometimes for months, before I could begin to bring their system into a properly functioning state. In fact, people would not only need a variety of supplements, but also physical therapies alongside a lot of colour therapy, too. In these early days, I had to wait for a photo to be sent that I would put in a light box and place on a windowsill for anything up to two weeks, or more. But one day, a client contacted me in a very distressed state needing a quicker response. I then remembered the electric light box from my colour training which transmitted a treatment in twenty minutes! That was the beginning of doing colour treatment via electric light. It's a truly amazing therapy which goes back to the times of the Ancient Egyptians and their temples of colour. As we shall later see, colour is also very much linked to all the notes of the musical scale. I would like to pay a tribute here to Marie Louise Lacy, my colour therapy tutor. Her book *Know Yourself through Colour* may still be available.

In order to end this chapter on a lighter note, when I was giving colour therapy through natural light, I would often wake up to find little green slugs had taken up residence inside the Light Boxes! They must have climbed up the outside walls, feeling rather detested by gardeners, to at last find a little slug haven. How amazing to be drawn to colour in this way!

CHAPTER 10

In solitude and peace
Think deeply
I am you and you are me
Only space lies
Between us

Larry Winters
(Larry Winters died in 1977 from an overdose in Barlinnie Prison.)

So, what was happening during this period in my "silent relationship"?

A lady rang me who called herself a clairvoyant astrologer. She was interested to know more about the healing work I was doing, but quickly started to tell me things about my unusual relationship. She referred to it as the "Twin Soul" connection I had read about in the book by St Germain. We are only now beginning to understand it better, for certain situations may not be quite what we think. Relationships, as Eckhart Tolle reminds us, have always provided a special opportunity for conscious evolvement although they may, in fact, play an even more important role as time goes by. However, to go back to the astrologer, she maintained that our relationship would be eternal despite the current difficulties. An "establishment" background was tearing him apart and he was desperately seeking a solution. St Germain explains this in these terms;

> *"The body of energy of you that is femaleness has within it many different diversions of frequencies of the spectrum of Light. As the one particular frequency which you perceive as yourself has a resonance, there is a corresponding resonance*

in the male body of energy. This is your "twin flame". All the
rest of them are your soul mates. The two of them together
ignite one another and transmute into wholeness and will
bring all of them together."

The astrologer hasn't been in contact again, so my belief is that she simply came to help further my understanding.

Shortly after this conversation, I became aware of a strange smell in my living room. At first I thought it might be coming from the chimney, but that was blocked off. I soon realised the smell was all around me and I then had the intuition that it might well be my twin soul's powerful troubled thought forms manifesting themselves.

In my healing work I have always given myself the guiding principle of not doing anything for anyone without their knowledge, even though I am often asked to. However, there are exceptions, of course, in the case of very sick people, or children and animals. I considered that this situation ought to be considered as an exception and I decided to try to help him. The smell diminished almost immediately. From then on I have been able to do distance work for him in the same way as everyone else.

This incident is one of many in which I was learning more and more about how thoughts can manifest themselves; I was exploring the power of THOUGHT. Another guiding principle that seemed to be a direct consequence of the first is that we may all learn to accept even the most unusual situations as being "right" for us at a particular moment. However, let us go back to another example of the power of thought.

A client sent me a book about the life of the inventor Nikola Tesla, who is only just gaining recognition for his work with the AC electrical current used by innumerable modern day appliances. He had a rather eccentric personality, made his first million before he was forty, but died almost destitute. He never had a close relationship, but grew to love pigeons and was heartbroken when one particular pigeon died. For some reason, my client felt I needed to read about him. I looked to see whether Tesla had reached the Higher dimensions since his death in 1943 and found that he hadn't. I then remembered having had personal experience with the death of a small pigeon on my patio some years ago to whom I dedicated a poem called "Intimate Passing" in my book *Over The Rainbow*. My recollections seemed to have created a connection between us, for when I looked again at Tesla, all he needed was pink colour healing for love and he was then able to move into the light.

A family friend had died recently with many unresolved relationship conflicts. He had been a poet at heart and a great admirer of Robert Burns, a fellow Scotsman. He had told me about his love of the "Lea Rigg" which happens to be one of the songs in my repertoire for the harp. Pondering on the way, I seemed to have created a link with Tesla I decided to play and sing my arrangement of the "Lea Rigg". I was later amazed to find that my friend also needed the same pink colour healing after which he was also then able to move on to higher realms.

It seems to be very important for people to be able to bring significant things to a conclusion within the Earth dimension. I shall come back to this subject again later.

CHAPTER 11

Darest thou now, O Soul
Walk out with me towards the unknown region.
Where neither ground is for the feet nor any path to follow
No map there nor guide…
All is black before us
Till, when the ties loosen
All but the ties eternal, Time and Space
Nor darkness, gravitation, sense, nor any bounds bounding us
Then we burst forth, we float
In time and space, O Soul prepared for then.
Equal equipt at last (O joy O fruit of All)
Thus to fulfil, O Soul…

Walt Whitman - poet

What lovely words from Walt Whitman, to express the nature of this evolving journey for humanity.

In 2008, a client came to me, aged just fifty, needing regeneration at a level I would usually be giving an elderly person. I thought it might just be a "one off" case but no, one person after another followed, of all age groups. After regeneration, they all needed white powder gold which can only be described as having an alchemical effect on the cells of the body transmuting them into a higher state. This treatment was followed in turn by the call for certain minerals in a specific order: boron, silicon, chromium, copper, manganese, strontium and fluorine. The planetary rise in vibration was most certainly having a definite effect now on the human body. This would culminate in what I would qualify as being one of the biggest events in our human history.

In December 2009, I started to detect a complete change in people's glandular system. Up to this date, the irregularities would have been quite predictable, usually caused by the ancestral bloodline imprints and/or what I term our "own agenda". However, I began to observe that these irregularities were being spontaneously corrected, but that, on the other hand, at the brain level, the pineal gland had started to become active, hence creating imbalance.

Western science has never known much about the pineal gland, apart from the fact that on death it becomes calcified. It is from eastern sources we learn that it has always been actively involved during the period of puberty after which it goes back into a dormant state again.

Before going any further, I would like to comment on the fact that the changes in the glandular system observed in December 2009 didn't just happen "out of the blue". Everything that happens on our planet is governed by natural laws. As previously mentioned, the vibrational rate on Earth has been rising since around 1987 caused by an event that has become known as the Harmonic Convergence. On August 16th, 1987 the Harmonic Convergence marked the fulfilment of the Mayan prophecy attributed to Quetzalcoatl according to José Argüelles' interpretation of the Mayan calendar. This date also corresponded with an exceptional astrological alignment, called the trine, of the sun, the moon and 6 out of the 8 planets. This event was celebrated by the first globally synchronised meditation in many parts of the world and is, to quote José Argüelles, "the point at which the counter-spin of history finally comes to a momentary halt and the spin of still imperceptible post-history commences". I will return later to this subject, but to go back to my work it has obviously taken all the interim years before we could start to see how the human body was to be affected.

This having been said, may we now pick up the thread and go back to the course of the exciting events that were unfolding. A few weeks later, the pituitary gland, which is the master gland, had also become unstable in every client I looked at. Having been very involved with an eastern spiritual master, I was well aware of what this may imply for the human race. Evidence seemed to point to the fact that, by an act of grace, humanity was ready to make an evolutionary leap in consciousness. The awakening of the pineal gland and its subtle counterpart, the third eye, means that with ancestral baggage released, we can begin to evolve from a fragmented state into integration. It seems we have been given an "opportunity" to start again with a fresh slate once we have gone through, what I call, a "clean-up operation". In other words, to use an analogy, it is a bit like having a problem on the car for a long time which has caused a lot of knock on effects. The engineer tells us he has finally discovered the root cause, but we now have to deal with all the other problems it has caused. To a certain extent, this is rather like the event that has occurred in our human bodies. Every human being has undergone a change in the glandular system. Since it is our regulating system, it was obvious, as far as I was concerned, that it was going to have a profound effect on us. Many people have known about the planetary shift, but unless one has been working at this high energetic level, probably more understood by quantum physicists, it is difficult to appreciate the consequences. I haven't yet talked to anyone who really realises how this major event is beginning to change the whole human body and how it is altering the necessary tools that will be needed to help people from now on, from both orthodox and complementary sources. Unless the whole situation is fully apprehended, it is likely to cause many problems as I will explain.

I have observed two major effects of this change in the body's regulating system. The first one can be on a physical level. More and more people began to complain of unusual headaches, dizziness, vision problems, blocked ears, issues around the heart area, breathing difficulties, erratic body temperature and blood pressure, a lot of digestive problems, aches and pains mysteriously manifesting and, oh, excessive tiredness, to name just the main issues people talk about!

The other big change is on the level of relationships. Over time, our "baggage", or unfinished business, has been played out as described previously. However, from this point onwards, I started to observe how people seemed to express deeper and deeper insights about themselves.

In 2010, I began to pick up the need for a certain quartet of colour healing: blue, pink, lavender and magenta. Blue is for self expression, pink for love, lavender for grief and magenta or ultra-violet/infra-red is all to do with fine chemical changes going on at a cellular level. Not long after this, I found that everybody needed a very specific therapy, the Metamorphic Technique. Without going into too much detail, this technique deals with all sorts of pre-birth issues. It has been around since the late 80s, but I had never picked it up for anybody before now. Little by little, I began to find that everyone seemed to require this specific therapy. I had the distinct impression that the quartet of colours mentioned before were very closely linked to this technique. A very "tuned in" client told me that the term "cellular integration chamber" had kept coming into her mind as I commented on the need for the Metamorphic Technique to be preceded by this particular quartet of colours.

Gradually, I was coming across so many people requiring the same healing at the same time that it appeared impractical, if not impossible, to do things individually. I considered that the only reasonable way forward seemed to explore the possibility of collective healing through thought. I discovered the Russians had been researching this for ten years, apparently regenerating organs surgically removed through the power of thought. Why not? Thought is indeed beyond the speed of light. Our scientists will gradually catch up!

I decided to give it a try and right from the outset "collective" healing through thought gave good results. So much so, I subsequently started to do individual healing this way.

Before we move on to my healing work through thought, I'd like to explore this concept in a deeper way.

CHAPTER 12

How you feel in any one moment is more important than anything else, because how you feel right now is creating your life.

The Power by Rhonda Byrne

Because of my "silent communication" for so many years, I've become very aware of the power of thought and the effect it can have on our bodies since the mind and the body have such an intricate link. Now that my collective work for so many people could only be possible through the power of thought, it is interesting to say a few words about the huge effect that thought has on our everyday lives, so we can consciously begin to take on more and more responsibility for our own destiny.

Ralph Waldo Trine wrote on this subject 100 years ago in *In Tune with the Infinite*, the subtitle being "Fullness of Peace, Power and Plenty". Right at the beginning he says:

"within yourself lays the cause of whatever enters your life. To come into the full realization of your own awakened interior powers is to be able to condition your life in exact accord with what you would have it... Thoughts are forces subtle, vital, creative continually building and shaping our lives according to their nature. It is in this way that the life always and inevitably follows the thought... The optimist is right. The pessimist is right. The one differs from the other as the light from the dark. Yet both are right. Each is right from his own particular point of view, and this point of view is the determining factor in the

*life of each. It determines as to whether it is a life of power or
of importance, of peace or of pain, of success or of failure."
Talking of bodily vigour he goes on to say that "practically all
disease with its consequent suffering has its origin in perverted
mental and emotional states and conditions... We should keep
a high ideal of health and harmony constantly in mind..."*

The important influence of the mind-over-matter is now generally accepted
as is the role of the psyche in promoting and maintaining good health. The
nature of my own work often includes having to deal with the harmful
effects of negative thoughts. One of the most impressive consequences can
be seen in people who leave this life in a state of mental turmoil.

Having the ability, by thought, to make contact with any of my clients
who have died, I have observed, by the nature of the colour therapy that
they still need, how devastated many people are when they realise that
they have lost the opportunity to accomplish whatever they came into this
incarnation to achieve. Of course, there have always been the more evolved
souls who manage to fulfil their "contract" and do indeed move straight on
to the Higher realms. However, it is not the case for the huge majority and
this is one of the main reasons why so much "spirit attachment" takes place.
People are so troubled at death that they attach themselves to the living,
feeding off their energy fields or, in other cases, they remain in places they
were familiar with during their earthly life.

As we evolve we become aware that it is not our birthright to suffer to
this extent. Changing our understanding, our way of thinking, means that
we can really create the existence we desire. Being aware of this offers a
whole new perspective on the future that lies before us.

Going back to Ralph Waldo Trine, his words describe so perfectly the
power of thought:

*There are loyal hearts, there are spirits brave
There are souls that are pure and true
Then give to the world the best you have
And the best will come back to you*

This is a very positive expression of the old adage *"whatever we sow, that shall we also reap."* By putting hatred into the world, we make it a literal hell! Put love into the world, and heaven with all its beauties and glories will become a reality. The time will come when the work of physicians will not be to treat the body, but to heal the mind. With all this important understanding let us now take up the thread of the description of the evolving events of my healing journey via the power of thought.

CHAPTER 13

*The manifest Universe is continually expanding and will go
on expanding eternally in the Infinite Universe, never ceasing.
Through your experience in this plane of action, so you are
able to help in this expansion*
Divine Healing of Mind and Body (The Jesus lectures)
by M. Macdonald Bayne

Around the same time as it had become necessary to begin "collective"
healing through thought, alongside my individual healing, a client sent me
an article that discussed the work now being done in some pain clinics
into the nature of physical pain and how they were moving towards the
understanding that all physical pain had an emotional content.

Again we turn to sources quoted by Henry Maudsley in 1918:

*The sorrow that has no vent in tears may make other organs
weep. When our habitual ways of coping are overwhelmed
we are capable of somaticising psychological pain. In such
cases the mind senses that the emotions are too painful to
experience, so it attempts to protect the psyche. Experiencing
the pain physically, as terrible as it may feel, is more tolerable
than feeling the depth of the psychological pain.*

I do agree with Henry Maudsley to the extent that I came to consider
emotional pain as probably being one of the biggest problems for human
beings! After much reflection, I felt that it probably wouldn't be possible for
people to deal with such unconscious situations, and so I decided I would

"ask" for the emotional pain to be released on a collective level.

Little did I realise, at that time, that I would have to be doing this six times a day for the next six months! Over this period the pain did seem to lessen, and as the general anxiety reduced everyone seemed to require a specialised product called zeolite, which is a mineral complex created from molten lava as it pours into and reacts with the sea. Zeolite has potent healing effects, having an alchemical combination of the elements: air, earth, water and fire. Its unique structure acts like a magnet drawing toxins to itself. In parallel to this "zeolite phase" I also learned that the active astrological planets, at this time, were associated with the elements air, earth, water and fire! As in the heavens above, so it was on the Earth beneath! The collective need for zeolite persisted for several weeks. It was as though clearing the emotions had completely gunged up the physical body.

What was next?

Well, a client was talking to me about some equipment he had come across on the internet: a vibro-acoustic apparatus that claimed to increase the local blood supply to neural fibres, tissues and nervous centres, thereby improving organ functions and blood quality. I discovered that this information in fact pointed the way towards the next line of action and I gave my clients the benefits of this apparatus, by thought, collectively over the following few weeks. It was during this same period, I was also constantly finding imbalance in the body Ph acid/alkaline.

Once this phase was completed the next collective stage was homeopathy which finished by attaining the MM potency of 66 MM. I'm sure homeopaths would rarely get up to MM.

Moving on, yet again, I was finding the need for a therapy known as AtlasPROfilax. This is usually done as a physical therapy to correct the top vertebrae in the spine. A Swiss man discovered that the spine is 23° misaligned. Although this is still rather a controversial theory, everyone crossing my path seemed to require it, but, by thought, and so I decided to give it collectively to all my clients past or present.

So where are we now?

Well, around about March 2011, I was again helped by a client who asked me if I could check her Assemblage Point, to see whether it was correctly aligned. This is the name given to the vortex of the surrounding energy field which is considered to be set in a healthy, stationary, nearly central position at around the age of seven in the case of children living in a stable home environment in which they can positively identify with their parent figures. If this is not the case, the Assemblage Point location remains unstable. It has also been determined that the Assemblage Point is associated with the biological activity of all the organs and glands including the brain. Everybody coming to me needed this to be realigned as part of the initial individual healing process, even though many came from what they considered to be a stable home environment. The need for realignment could be due to the aforementioned planetary shift in energy, and since the body is undergoing so much change, the Assemblage Point location tends to become unbalanced. The technique of realignment has been available as a physical therapy for a number of years, but again I do this by thought.

I was amazed to discover that the next period of healing involved all the 32 teeth in our mouths which are linked to every part of the body via meridians. I would often hear clients say, "Well, I've lost a lot of teeth."

Before going any further, it may be interesting to point out that when working at this kind of level, one is working at an energy field far beyond the physical and so whether teeth are still actually present is not an issue! I realised this a long time ago when dealing with the removal of other body parts and its overall effect on the glandular system. A good example is the case of a limb that has been amputated, perhaps a leg. One obviously needs a leg to walk on in this dimension, but if at the energy level healing has taken place then the body can still function energetically. One of the things that many orthodox people do not take into consideration is that any physical intervention interferes with the unseen organising energy field thus weakening the physical body parts.

How symbolic that the next phase on this healing journey occurred in the spring, at Easter, a time of renewal. I had been rereading *Healing with Sound* by Olivea Dewhurst-Maddock and it came into my mind that sound could be the next stage, and indeed it turned out to be so. For those people who are not familiar with music, there are seven basic notes that can be repeated either higher or lower. All music is the different combination of these seven notes. When I looked, I found clients didn't just want the scale CDEFGAB, but needed them in a particular order. In other words notes that would play a specific tune! This went on for weeks and weeks since every note is linked to a different part of the physical body, and every note is also associated with the colours of the spectrum! Then some people started to require a different combination of notes. Eventually, all that was called for, day after day, was just one note: B, that is associated with every part of the physical body, the colour violet in the spectrum and the crown chakra. I came to the conclusion that the purpose of this journey was to bring our very "out of tune instrument", the body, into a beautifully tuned one, in resonance with the rest of the universe.

This notion of celestial harmony is also behind the well-established correlation between certain mathematical calculations and the sacred geometry of beautiful buildings such as Chartres cathedral or the layout of many picturesque masterpieces.

The darker side of the picture, as always, is that human beings have also been upsetting this subtle equilibrium in the universe by our misunderstood power of thought!

This stage came to a timely end, since from reliable sources we have been informed that the planetary rise in energy was brought to a particular completion in the middle of August 2011 and this would consequently bring about the opening of the heart centre in human beings.

Prior to this August event, the need to clear past life issues via the Metamorphic Technique had been presenting itself with greater and greater urgency and in the end, I had to deal with the situation collectively, by thought, sometimes as frequently as every half an hour throughout the day! Fortunately, since the event in August, no more past life issues have been observed other than the initial session that completes the individual healing process for everybody now coming to me. This is an essential preliminary for everyone in order to move through a sort of "gateway" into this new level of consciousness being granted to humanity. However, I was not very surprised to then pick up a specific homeopathic remedy to address the heart centre in connection with this same event.

There was now an important stage for human beings to be involved in. Homeopaths have always understood what is known as Miasms. For those of us who may not be familiar with the term Miasms are *"an inherent weakness in man's subtle constitution, which, as part of karma, can be infiltrated by a disease pattern derived from past Earth-plane activity."* This can lead to a break out in contagious, infectious physical forms and has been one of the explanations of the cause of all chronic health conditions. Without going into too much detail, let us say there are different Miasms, and some can go back 25 million years!

For two months, I was clearing the release of Miasms from clients sometimes up to eight times a day with homeopathic potencies finishing up at the amazing potency of 373 MM!

Emotional pain release followed for days, along with much colour healing: Lavender for grief, pink for love and magenta, trying to keep our seesaw in balance! A particular mineral needed collectively was magnetite that has a crystalline content. Gradually, on a daily basis, everyone collectively needed zinc along with white powder gold, or liquid manna that contains white powder gold. This latter supplement is described as refined monatomic elements (single atoms of elements). An alchemical process on the mineral powder to extract the monatomic elements is then suspended in frequency charged water to keep them in a high spin state. Laurence Gardener discusses this extensively in his 2003 book *Lost Secrets of the Sacred Ark* in which he describes the incredible power of gold.

Following on from magnetite has been diamond

Not by chance, as I was looking to see what might help a client with facial hair, I discovered the homeopathic remedy was connected to diamond! The explanation is the following: "The spiritual body contains many diamond based Tetrahedral forms (known in Platonic Solids, explained later) that become integrated with the carbon of the physical body. This effectively reverses aging and enables the process of evolvement. Humanity partially maintains a crystalline configuration within its skeleton, blood and immune systems. Crystalline bodies facilitate the ability to channel transfer and generally communicate between the different dimensions of reality."

This brings us up to autumn 2011. Many people believe that the 11th November, 2011, was the following significant entry into the new era for planet Earth. Immediately prior to that event, I noticed we were still needing collective release of residual emotional pain for over 24 hours until, at 11.30am the day of the 11th November, everybody suddenly needed pink healing for love, how wonderful, as though the divine guidance was giving all of us a big hug!

A few days after this love vibration on an individual, and occasionally collective, level a big need appeared for lavender colour healing. It was as though the emotional content had been dealt with, but what still seemed to linger was the outwardly manifested unhappiness and sorrow. I was becoming convinced that whatever the physical symptoms, the root cause is always unhappiness.

In the same way as zeolite was needed 18 months before, to cleanse the physical body following release of the emotional vibration, so at this later stage the lavender colour healing was followed by a massive collective call for purification through indigo and yellow colour healing. After millions of years, this is probably the first time our physical bodies have been at such a high level of functioning. Furthermore, what we have to attend to now is how our thinking minds can create either happiness or unhappiness, as Ralph Waldo Trine reminded us so long ago!

And on the subject of happiness, I always find it helpful to remember my spiritual master's suggestion that if we have had five minutes not feeling good, then think of something uplifting for the next 10 minutes. In that way, we keep our "bank balance out of the red"! We cannot expect to achieve things all in one go.

I do like to remind people of other words that my spiritual master said. First and foremost, ACCEPTANCE of where we are at the time, for if we don't accept things we will continue to suffer. Then we must constantly ASK, in any way appropriate, for help and lastly, of course, trust the whole process.

INTERLUDE

I am the seed of the wild poppy
And the grasses that cover the hills
I am the breath of the vagrant things that move in quiet places
And the Source of the streams that nourish the valley.
I am the voice of the wind and that of the gull that screams before it
I am the first light of the morning
And the darkness of the hour that precedes it.
I am all things that are, that have been, that shall be.
Yet in all things am I lost for I am (no-thing) nothing.
Seek not to love me, for I am not to be sought after,
But in that still moment of thoughtlessness
I am there
In that moment I am Man aware.

The Infinite Man Winston Cooper

CHAPTER 14

The challenge is to dissolve the old pattern of thought and perception, rather than try to contradict it, control it or destroy it by force or will...

David Bohm, physicist

So, what has been happening in the countryside while the high-speed train has been whizzing along?

Well, quite a lot. The physical body is now up to the highest level of functioning that it has been capable of over the course of millions of years. One of the most direct consequences, and the one I am particularly interested in, is that we shall probably discover that 99% of all the healing systems and therapies will no longer be appropriate. Orthodox practitioners may become unsuitable since it is difficult to foresee how all the massive changes have altered the regulation of the human body. I am already seeing how clients are creating difficulties for the medical profession when it comes to diagnosis. Even in the alternative healing field, feathers are beginning to be ruffled when I am finding that clients have reached this high level state and apparently need nothing else. On the contrary, I have seen how the energy field can temporarily "shut down" if they carry on with inappropriate healing methods. This is another one of the times of great change that humanity has undergone in the course of its history, but I feel confident that as certain doors close others will open up as time goes by.

On a daily basis I am observing that when new clients come to me they don't seem to have to go through all the stages I have talked about since the beginning of December 2009. Once the initial individual irregularities have been dealt with, and after a session of the Metamorphic Technique, they then seem to be able to come in to the collective healing at whatever stage it has reached. It would seem that all the stages that everyone has gone through individually since December 2009 have not only been beneficial for themselves, but also for others on the planet. In this case we can be amazed to discover the "Divine Plan" that is taking place. We could also interpret the situation from another point of view. Human beings, having dealt with their individual issues, are given the opportunity to be part of new evolving humanity. In just two years, clients have gone from needing supplements by mouth to being able to receive treatment by light, and from now on through thought.

The world of crystals has also changed. Left inside houses they tend to close down. Put outside they come back to life. I feel that this may be a way of helping the surrounding environment.

Some of my clients are telling me that they are starting to feel uncomfortable amongst the social groups they have been mixing with for years. I interpret this as an inevitable incompatibility at a vibrational level as the planet goes through this transitional stage. The need for relative isolation often precedes, or follows, fundamental changes, and at the high end of the scale, all the great spiritual masters of the past have gone through periods of complete isolation and inner reflection. There is a Buddhist saying: Isolation - Breakthrough - Transformation.

Going back, once again, to the situation of those who have died, I have noticed that there seems to be less spirit attachment, although it can still be found especially in older houses, but here again it is possible that spirits may be starting to feel uncomfortable in the high vibrational atmosphere. More and more clients are mentioning how their deceased loved ones seem to be constantly "on their minds". As I have already said, I can discover whether someone who has left this dimension is still in conflict or ready to move on to higher dimensions. Apparently the vibrational changes on the planet are not having any effect on the fact that still very few manage to move on by themselves. However, I am now suggesting that my clients who are in this personal situation may like to see their loved ones into higher realms, or to help resolve issues if an entity is still in conflict. I can do the initial divining to see what the situation is and I am often asked to confirm a positive outcome. The majority of people are delighted to be able to do something and I think it is all helping to bring "completion" to the planet as we evolve higher. We will come back later on to the subject of communication between different dimensions.

Of course, all these exciting new changes are only apparent for a small minority. James Redfield, in his latest book *The Twelfth Insight*, reminds us to begin using our conversation in a conscious way. I can mention an example taken from my own experience. Amongst a group of people the conversation had got around to talking about the usual aches and pains. My contribution was that I was in perfect health, whereupon the response was, "Well you are indeed very fortunate." "No," I replied, "It isn't a question of luck, I know how to achieve this!"

"Ask and it shall be given". *"Seek and ye shall find"*. These are sayings based on ancient laws of the universe. We could also ponder a new way of considering another ancient adage. *"Many are called but few are chosen"*. In fact, it could be that many were called but few were able to choose! However, from now on, divinity has given every human being the same opportunity.

CHAPTER 15

A sphere, which is as many thousand
Solid as crystal, yet through all its
Flow, as through empty space, music and light
Ten thousand orbs involving and involved
Purple and azure, white and green and golden
... thousand sightless axles spinning...

P.B. Shelley, poet 1819

Let us continue to explore how our evolution is so much part of a vast interconnected whole.

Theo Gimble in his book *Healing through Colour* chooses the above quote to set the scene for his explanation of how the origins of matter have passed through various stages of density into final manifestation. In the course of this interplay, colour is the highest vibration, then comes sound and finally form.

As Marie Louise Lacey writes in *Know Yourself Through Colour:*

> *"as we evolve we shall know more and more about the power of colour, which is received through eye sensors known as rods, sensitive to low levels of light while those known as cones require a greater intensity of light and are sensitive to colour. The area in the centre of the retina has the highest concentration of cones and these produce sharp colour images while the rest of the retina contains mainly rods."*

She talks about the language of colour. Each has a different wavelength and vibration functioning on three levels: light, chemistry and sensation. The chemistry involves pigments and compounds. Therapists are more concerned with the other aspects. The rainbow spectrum affects the body physically, mentally and spiritually. Physically it moves up from the lower parts of the body through red, orange and yellow associated with the will, feelings and thought, to the higher aspects of Divine Wisdom, Divine Love and Divine Will through blue, indigo and violet. Individually, red is associated with courage, orange with health, yellow with wisdom, green with peace and harmony, blue with inspiration, indigo with intuition and violet with spiritual power.

We shall begin to understand that the lower vibrations, associated with red, are especially linked to important but more peripheral aspects of life. In order to attain deeper understanding, we need to move onto higher vibrations associated with the colour violet and its purifying, cleansing action which helps us to search for all that is noble, pure and divine. This quest for meaning in our lives involves giving more thought to choice in everyday aspects such as clothes, decor, illumination and, of course, food!

Kirlian photography has opened up another level of understanding allowing us to see the energy field around our bodies known as the aura. We can actually observe how disease changes the colours in the aura three weeks before manifesting in the physical body. We can also observe how the intensity of colour changes according to the state of our life force. When we are healthy the colours are bright and full of energy, but when they are dull they suggest a decline in energy. Photographers have even shown how meditation has a positive affect on the energy of the aura.

The late C.W. Leadbeater, a renowned theosophist and author of *Man Visible and Invisible* shows how emotions and thought patterns can also influence the aura. I myself had a personal experience of this when I went to visit the well-known Avatar Mother Meera. On approaching her, I saw a beautiful golden luminescence all around her head area.

Colour also extends into the field of numerology to the extent that every number is associated with a certain colour and is part of the reading I often do for clients since it reveals our life path, growth cycle stage and full potential.

Another theosophical publication, *Music Forms* by Geoffrey Hodson, shows lovely pictures of the shapes and colours clairvoyantly seen while certain music is played (for example Handel's *Messiah*.)

Returning to Marie Louise Lacy, she reminds us of the basic physics of colour and the fact that a red flower, for example, is seen as red because that particular flower absorbs all the other colours except red which is reflected back. In other words, that flower has a particular frequency of energy that makes us perceive it as being red. As our own vibrations of energy increase, we will probably be able to distinguish new shades or hues. Our perception of colour will gradually become "enlightened". What a fascinating perspective to dream about!

The next density of vibration after colour is Sound.

CHAPTER 16

The human body is a living manifestation of ratios and proportions. It is a "sounding board" awaiting the positive influences of therapeutic sounds in which pitch and volume, resonance and harmony play vital roles. We are an integral part of the unique and consistent geometry of our planet demonstrated by life forces and consciousness. We are part of and respond to the music of Gaïa.

Healing with Sound by Olivea Dewhurst Maddock

At the beginning there was light... but there was also sound. Animals, water, thunder, lightning, fire... In the bid to survive, but also to understand, foresee and control, specific sounds were used to attract prey or give alert, for example. However, even in difficult conditions or perhaps because of them, early man had the need to find purpose, to appease the elements and to embellish life. According to his physical surroundings and environment he made music with bone flutes, primitive drums and conch seashells without forgetting handclapping and probably chanting, the most primitive form of singing. The tribal drums and xylophones of Africa, the sacred rhythm of American Indian drums, the earthy powerful didgeridoo... Were they connecting to the fundamental primal sound of the universe? In later ancient societies music played an ever important role. The metallic Egyptian trumpets, or the sistrum shaken to open hearts to the gods, the Greek harps and song are just a few examples. Music combined to make sense and order and to allow connection with the higher powers.

David Tame, writing in his book *The Secret Power of Music*, states that:

"in ancient times sound itself, the very basis of all music, was thought to be ultimately related in some way to non-physical and sacred dimensions or places of existence. Audible sound was considered to be but an earthly reflection of a vibrational activity taking place beyond the physical world."

He goes on to say that the basic concept of "as in music, so in life" prevailed in one form or another throughout human civilisation. However, the spiritual or philosophical notion of music as a force capable of changing the individual and society has gradually moved towards a more commercial concept! Ancient civilisations believed music embodied within its tones, elements of the celestial order which govern the entire universe. There was a fundamental primal sound synonymous to what the Hindus call "Om" which was differentiated into twelve lesser sounds or tones. Furthermore, the Hindus believed that each of the twelve tones was associated with one of the twelve zodiacal regions of the heavens and in many lands astrology began in ancient times as the study of cosmic tones. On a more everyday level, performing music often came in conjunction with ceremony.

Evolved people over the past 2000 years have recognised that music is more than just entertainment. It is a noble art, a royal road to Higher appreciation and, as such, we may like to begin to select our music with this in mind. Corinne Heline, a New Age pioneer, suggests *"we shall see how it can become a principal source of healing for many individual and social ills!"* She also maintains, as we have said before, that virtually every major ancient civilisation held that music possessed the ability to transform and improve, or degrade, that civilisation.

Pythagoras (570–495(?)BC) the famous ancient Greek philosopher was also a wise teacher. Although the precise contribution of Pythagoras is unknown, since he did not leave any written record, later followers say he taught his students how certain musical chords and melodies produce definite responses within the human organism and demonstrated how a certain sequence of sounds played musically on an instrument can change behaviour patterns and accelerate healing. He was probably one of the first to discover that all music could be reduced to numbers and mathematical ratios and that the entire universe and all the phenomena therein could also be explained in these same terms.

Olivea Dewhurst Maddock reminds us how sound frequencies are tools for transformation. Some of the great master musicians and composers have had the very special destiny to bring to the human race all of the important and beneficial harmonies of sound. Their inspiration was in accordance with the general vibrational level of the planet at their time. In the long continuum of everlasting change even the fundamental building blocks of sound will continue to evolve, for example, through specific techniques such as the art of "toning" which uses the voice to allow us to express our own life force energies.

And on the subject of frequencies, the "Solfeggio tones" were one of the subjects discussed in *Healing Codes for the Biological Apocalypse* by Dr Leonard Horowitz and Dr Joseph Puleo.

The book describes how Joseph Puleo explores some of the mathematical theories of Pythagoras, the famous philosopher and mathematician. He also felt "guided" to the book of Numbers and discovered a pattern of repeating codes which he considered to be six sound frequencies.

As is well known, Hebrew letters are also numbers that have always been studied by the Kabbalah, the esoteric branch of Judaism. This is, in fact, the second branch of numerology alongside the Pythagorean method we may know more about.

Puleo suggests a possible relationship with the St John the Baptist hymn that is traditionally considered to be the origin of the names of the musical notes used in what the English call the tonic sol-fa system.

At the turn of the 11th century Guido d'Arezzo, in Italy, imagines a method to help monks to remember their plain chants. He took the first syllable of each verse of the famous St John the Baptist hymn to represent the six successive notes of the scale so that each note was sung one degree higher than the first syllable of the line that preceded it. As each syllable ended with a vowel sound they were particularly suitable for vocal use (it later became more common to use Do in the place of Ut, for the same reasons) the scale thus became UT (Do), RE, MI, FA, SOL and LA, (the SI came much later.)

These names for the musical notes are still used in France, Italy, Spain, Portugal, Russia and other European countries, whereas the Anglo Saxon countries have kept the system using letters C, D, E, F, G, A, B although many use a "Tonic Sol-fa method" when singing, as did my father!

Thanks to Guido d'Arezzo and a long line of dedicated monks, we have a well-recorded idea of the original plain chants, also helped by monasteries that have kept the unchanged tradition alive over the centuries.

Since Puleo's book was published back in 1999, much controversy has existed as to the way a specific hertz frequency could be associated with the notes as far back as the 11th century. Heinrich Rudolf Hertz (1857–1894), a German physicist was the first to artificially produce electromagnetic waves to very precise frequencies.

Nowadays, we have electronic tuners, but for many centuries there was no "international tuning system" and no way to verify that a particular song was sung at a specific pitch. Or rather, thanks to musical research on old instruments we know that each instrument maker, village, town or country had their own idea of tuning. This was not too much of a problem until musicians started to play together with different, complementary parts (polyphony) and as music evolved, instruments and tuning techniques had to follow. The first tuning fork appeared in 1711, and even then its duplication was done by ear…

Gregorian chanting was unaccompanied, "a capella", and although organs existed, to give a "first note", as already said each was tuned differently. However, although exact frequencies of sound could not have been precisely measured in hertz, the harmony of intervals was well known. One can hear the different harmonies, the perfect fifth, the perfect fourth, the octave etc. by listening to the vibration of a chord. In fact, the description of their exact ratios is attributed to Pythagoras, who apparently also had good ears! Middle age music has recently somewhat come back "into fashion" especially for the uplifting effects of its perfect intervals.

However, to return to Puleo and Horowitz, they state very clearly at the end of their book that due to the authors' limited knowledge of music, cryptography, ancient astrology, astrophysics and mathematics, the coded segments, Pythagorean patterns and numerical formulations provide a perfunctory beginning for investigators to pursue more in-depth studies. To a certain extent, I feel that my work using the solfeggio tones could be considered to be part of this investigation since it has been very important for me to know of these solfeggio frequencies. They have been part of the healing journey for many months replacing the ordinary scale I was using before.

Dr Lee Lorenzen, a world renowned biochemist working with water crystallisation methods to rejuvenate DNA, is said to have indicated that *"the 528 Hz frequency is well known to scientists working on DNA repair… We believe it may be beneficial in delaying aging process"*

Having said all this, what are we left with? Sound!

Sound has always been used as a vehicle towards the Divine. According to Christian and Hindu traditions, the universe was created directly from a Divine utterance; the OM which became the first Mantra, Aum. In the west, the Aum became Amen and the mantra took the form of a prayer.

Paying attention to the harmonics of sound is an ancient tradition, as for the Tibetan monks who have developed singing techniques that are very rich in harmonics. Tibetan bowls, or the beautiful Indian tempura, also produce rich harmonics and these chants and instruments are incorporated into spiritual practice. Harmonics are used to enrich music and raise the soul.

Today, there are many styles of music and at least as many opinions as how to produce sounds which will touch, heal, or spiritually uplift us. There are also a hundred-and-one ideas (especially on the internet!) on how the different qualities of sound and music may be combined to establish a link to the Divine and/or for therapeutic use in which sound has also been connected to other sources of knowledge such as quantum physics, fractals, sacred numerology and modern brainwave research.

The scientist Andrew Gladzewski did considerable research into correlations between such phenomena as atomic patterns, plants and harmonies in music. One of his conclusions was that *"atoms are harmonic resonances."* Other scientists, too, are beginning to regard the atom *"as a kind of tiny musical note."* Exploration has gone further now with many atomic physicists talking about *"exotic resonance"* and how we might discover and understand the quintessential nature of matter. In a book *Das Universum Singt* the German Wilfred Krüger seems to have demonstrated that the structure of the atom contains ratios and numbers which resemble to a degree impossible to account for by chance, the harmonic principles of music.

As music is understood from this deeper perspective inevitably the whole approach to teaching and performing could change.

Herbert Whone in *The Hidden Face of Music* published in 1984 says:

> *"It is the player who in a few short bars can cut through the dead skin of theoretical music and transport a listener to a state of vibrant awareness. Through his instrument he can play upon a more subtle instrument, the very human being that makes up his audience but first of all he has to become as dynamic as the universe in which he lives and this involves knowing and mastering the contents of his own Being. To learn to perform on any instrument involves a process of sensitivity that leads to the outer and inner instrument becoming One… man can become priest and musician of his own temple."*

The late Ravi Shankar, the great Sitar player often talked about how in ancient India the musicians were not only great performers but also advanced Yogis.

I can envisage a time when people again recognise the significance of their deeper integrated state as a starting point for learning an instrument or singing. Their music will carry a high range of harmonic frequencies and be performed in places, such as cathedrals, that embody the sacred geometric ratios.

Can we imagine such an event for musician and listener… complete interconnectedness…?

Healing with sound or music is a well known and documented realm, but have we ever thought how bees could play their part?

Valerie Solheim PhD decided to explore her intuition that if beehives were exposed to the amplified recording of selected healthy hive frequencies they might become more resilient to disease, pests, and environmental interference on a preventive, but also curative, level. She brings in the law of physics to explain how specific sound from one hive can elicit the same response from another hive.

Ancient civilisations around the Mediterranean, particularly the Egyptians, included spiritual practices founded on the beehive and some of the oldest shamanic practices in Northern Europe were based on veneration of the honey beehive. In fact, bees have the reputation of *"bringers of order"* and their hives served as models for the organisation of temples in many Mediterranean cultures. Their honeycombs are a series of perfect hexagons, a stable architectural form employed by nature in snowflakes, for example, for its strength and quality. It seems that the electromagnetic field created by the bee colony acts as an earth resonator. The sustained coherent sound emanating from the hive is archetypal, pure communication transmitted through vibration. When these sustained frequencies resonate through sacred geometric patterns, they create harmonic resonance within the core of our being from cell to spirit. Observation certainly suggests that this energy transfer is having a pronounced and positive effect on the hives, the environment and also the people in the area! What an exciting ongoing study!

And lastly, a little extra food for thought on the healing power of sound. Very recently, a well known musician died. While his music was being played on the radio as a tribute I found he was still in conflict. As the music continued he slowly responded to the pink colour vibration for love and was then able to move to the Higher realm by himself. His earthly life was thus completed.

CHAPTER 17

Looking upward the Sage contemplated the images in the heavens;
Looking downwards he observed the patterns on Earth

Fu Shi, First Emperor of China

Let us now move on to the final step through this universal world of matter, into the world of Form that we see all around us.

Sacred forms are found in nature, in the animal world, in nests and in cocoons and shells. Certain proportional ratios, called the Golden Mean, determine the growth patterns of shells and certain flowers. The curvature of the cochlea in the ear, the spiralling of water, antlers, human bones and even the human foetus develops to the constant music of these proportions. Shape and Form make a big impression on us in a psychological and therapeutic way. Specific mathematical proportions were understood by the ancients when they built such places as the pyramids, Stonehenge or the Hindu Temples.

Shapes determined by certain numbers actually trap, resonate and amplify specific modes of vibration and this sacred geometry and numerology are much more than purely symbolic. At this time even gemstones were cut to amplify resonance.

Man recognised this and, as his consciousness expanded, he built the places of worship inspired by the sacred order as in the celebrated gothic cathedrals. The famous rose windows, especially in Chartres Cathedral (the rose motif has always been a peace symbol), incorporates an important glass believed to be made by alchemists, a heavily guarded secret. The glassmakers' art reached its height in the 13th century and was gradually debased after this time.

"The Five Sacred Solids", known as the Platonic solids, are the five geometrical forms that can be inscribed within a sphere with all their apexes touching the sphere. Plato (427–347BC) identified them with the five elements that make up the world and associated them with the numbers 12345. The cube is associated with earth, the tetrahedron with fire, the octahedron with air, the icosahedron with water and the dodecahedron with the universe since it is composed of twelve regular pentagons corresponding to the signs of the zodiac. There are other figures such as the Vesica Piscis, the pentangle and the cross. With the complete vocabulary of shapes and proportions, artists and architects could create while transmitting specific meanings and qualities. For example, when some of these sacred geometric forms are superimposed over the ground plan of the Lady Chapel at Glastonbury, one can see some of the same forms, and symbolic proportions as those that were used at Stonehenge. They were therefore delivering a similar message. In fact, every object including the human body carries a unique proportion of all five shapes.

The Golden Mean, or Phi, is the proportion found in all nature, as already mentioned. Johannes Kepler, German astronomer (1571–1630) called this *"divine proportion"* for he discovered that *"when the platonic solids were inscribed within spheres and then within each other in sequence they described the orbits of the planets in the solar system"*. A few famous architects have used these proportions in modern times, the most well known being Le Corbusier and Frank Lloyd Wright.

As Prince Charles writes in his book *Harmony*, *"Each piece of sacred art or architecture was created according to the timeless principles of the grammar of harmony along with music and poetry in the method of achieving this since it comforts the heart rather than the head. The history of civilisation is much more interconnected than the history books suggest."* He has put theory to practice in his work with architects in Poundbury in the Dorset area of England.

A.T. Mann in his book *Sacred Architecture* explains that symbolism has often been disguised throughout history as an outer meaning for the masses and an inner meaning for the initiates since there was always concern that the true spiritual principles would be discovered and abused by those in power. Hence, in Egyptian religions, hieroglyphs and architecture incorporated a symbolic language. Jewish rabbis created the numerogical system called the Kabbalah. The Pythagoreans concealed their philosophy in numerology and geometry. The Gnostics used parables and poetry not only to communicate cosmic principles, but also to avoid being persecuted by the Orthodox Church. The true meaning of the symbols were understood by the "priesthood" and carefully kept secret from the uninitiated. Certain schools of artists and architects were trained by the priests to understand and communicate the symbolic through their work.

Alfred Watkins, (1855–1930) photographer, inventor and antiquarian with a vast interest in landscape suddenly had a great insight at the age of seventy into how the sacred monuments across Herefordshire were linked by a web of lines now known as Ley Lines which have very powerful force fields. There is a very important Ley Line that links Stonehenge stone circle to Salisbury Cathedral. It is now known that Ley Line traditions extend universally. Certainly the Chinese understood this when they developed the art and science of placing and orientating buildings according to "earth forces" called Feng Shui, literally *"wind and water"*. Other places of powerful energy lines are the Mexican Temples of the Sun and the Nazca lines in Peru.

Due to a lack of conscious awareness, we have not always built our houses on the best sites thus interrupting, in certain cases, this flow of energy. When new clients come to me one of the first things I do as part of the healing process is to check whether there is any imbalance of the earth energies associated with the property they live in, and rebalance, if necessary, by thought, for it can certainly affect the harmony of the people living there. I also cleanse and purify the atmosphere, too. Sometimes a property that has been difficult to sell can be due to this situation. Many of us can sense the atmosphere in a house right away.

Let's leave the last words of this chapter to A.T. Mann:

"The new sacred architecture begins with new architects. Only when architectural students are taught the mysteries, and magic of symbolism, astrology, mythology made real, and the reality of the sacred, will a new architecture arise like a phoenix from the ashes all around us."

However, leaving aside the subject of architecture other figures are being brought to our attention and will be discussed in the next chapter.

CHAPTER 18

The integrated whole mind will see one whole universe
The Secret of the Creative Vacuum, Man and the Energy Dance
by John Davidson

Let us now turn to a book called *The Bringers of the Dawn* by Barbara Marciniak who brings through teachings from the Pleiadians, a group of enlightened beings, otherwise described as a *"collective of energy"*. They started to remake their connections again to planet Earth more than 20 years ago now. They give us important information on the phenomenon of Crop circles... new forms.

Crop circles appear displaying geometrical forms and ancient religious symbols. Many people do not know what to make of them, while others believe that they are hoaxes, but in a very thoroughly researched book *Secrets in the Fields* the author, Freddy Silva gives evidence showing that most of the crop circles are genuine.

According to Barbara Marciniak

> *"These Language of Light geometric shapes and forms are collections of experiences of individuals who have incarnated on this planet... awakened themselves to high abilities and then manifested themselves as language and geometric components. Once, these energies existed as men and women on this planet. They have evolved themselves into geometric symbols, and they exist in their sphere of activity just like we exist in our body. These entities exist in a language system or a geometric system. There are universes of these systems*

and there are visitations into our own universe from those universes at this time. There are circles and other shapes being put upon this planet in the grain fields that are inexplicable as far as we are concerned. These imprints are a frequency...a song or story that is being implanted on the surface of Earth with language symbols...Many of the dwellings in the Pleiades do not have shapes as we know them and it is understood there that shapes and angles hold energy...we can learn to create these shapes and live in and around them. Energies are formed and transmitted this way."

She goes on to explain that energy portals on the planet are now open again, because in order for our consciousness to rise, energy needs to be housed on the planet itself. In the case of the crop circles, we also discover that the geometric shapes are put here by sound above our human frequency. Their shapes and forms are evolving, and they are all interconnected, carriers of intelligence from one continent to another.

It is my understanding that sacred geometry is really an evolved form of intelligence that can communicate huge amounts of information in much the same way as the ancient hieroglyphs. It will probably help activate the Earth's grid system. Everything is designed to show us that the reasoning mind cannot control all of the data! It is a trigger to encourage human beings to move beyond their limitations and begin to use a more *"feeling"* approach rather than the *"thinking"* one. The British are well known for having a very logical, down to earth consciousness! Although we might remember that the British Isles has a very ancient history that lies dormant within our archetypal, intuitive faculties. We must also note that none of the circles actually damage the wheat in the fields and it can still be harvested. A situation that is not too upsetting for the farmers and true to the legendary British sense of humour.

When I visited the community at Damanhur in Italy, which I describe in detail in my first book, I was fascinated by the way they use the spiral form which was widely employed by the Egyptians, Celts and in ancient Arabian civilisations. At Damanhur they call this "Selfica" and the practical objects that are developed from this ancient science are called "Selfs" They are frequently made from gold, silver and also copper and bronze and I always wear a lovely gold ring purchased while staying there.

However, to return to Freddy Silva… for much of his life he has been an art director and photographer but alongside his profession he has also been an ardent student of Earth mysteries and is considered to be one of the world's leading specialists on this phenomenon.

He describes how some researchers have gone a step forward, in conducting experiments trying to deliberately provoke glyph formation. For example, two people took up residence inside a crop circle and played music on stringed instruments. They observed a crackling sound and the next day found that a small formation of circles had appeared. Other glyphs appeared in neighbouring fields and the researchers were not sure how to interpret the results. Were the circle makers responding to the music, or was it the musicians and their thoughts which had provoked their formation? Or were these particularly sensitive people picking up forms that were already in the making? As in the case of a researcher who asked for a certain pattern to appear and fell asleep to dream of a Celtic cross design which indeed appeared on the land behind his house the next day!

Freddy Silva has also observed that the majority of the circles materialise between 2am and 3am when the Earth's electromagnetic field is at its lowest ebb.

This information can be somewhat related to another line of research initiated and led by Paul Devereux who sets out to investigate the belief, existing in folklore and modern anecdote that certain prehistoric sites around the country had unusual energies.

Using magnetometers, Geiger counters, ultra-sonic detectors to name, but a few "The Dragon Project", as it came to be known, detected consistently higher radiation counts, magnetic anomalies and unusual if not always consistent ultrasonic emissions from stone circles, and other ancient structures up and down the UK.

It is felt that there is a developing interactive communication. Isabelle Kingston, a very reliable channel has brought forward to us the following information.

"We have been coming for years and years to bring the power necessary to build the New Jerusalem. Your country lies in the centre of the great pyramid of light which encircles your world".

Is our ancient country, the *"green and pleasant land"* depicted by the visionary poet William Blake, holding the balance and the key to the world? The high pitched frequencies from the crop circles can create heightened states of awareness.

David Myers and David Percy are described as two people who have embarked on the road to new technological wonders described in their book "Two Thirds" a history of our galaxy. They provide stunning evidence of a number of crop glyphs encoding technology far beyond the present accepted boundaries of physics. Further information suggests our DNA may be in the process of changing.

Fifteen centuries of European history teaches us that if a great number of people hold an overtly pessimistic image of the future, that image will probable manifest as reality, a reminder, yet again, of the laws of attraction. Apocalypses are less the result of predictions, but more the release of pathological behaviour in society which creates the situation on the ground! With its foundations in Divine principles, the crop circle resurgence at this pivotal moment is precipitating change. After the birth of the new millennium we are already witnessing many more ideas based on hope, sustainability, spirituality and tolerance. For this change to be converted into action we must participate as co-creators. Another sober warning comes from further communications. *"You have a choice to muck your world up or make it a better place".* They are here to help if we need, but it is up to us. We have to abandon the idea that there is a saviour for our world. To quote a Hopi Elder, *"We are the ones we have been waiting for!"*

INTERLUDE

Three monkeys sat in a coconut tree
Discussing things as they're said to be.
Said one to the others, now listen you two,
There's a certain rumour that can't be true.
That man descended from our noble race
The very idea! T'is a dire disgrace!

No monkey ever deserted his wife,
Starved her baby and ruined her life
And you've never known a mother monk
To leave her baby with others to bunk,
Or pass them on from one to another
Till they hardly know who is their mother.

And another thing, you will never see,
A monk build a fence round a coconut tree
And let the coconuts go to waste
Forbidding all the other monks a taste.
Why, if I put a fence around this tree,
Starvation would force you to steal from me.

There's another thing a monk won't do,
Go out at night and get in a stew,
Or use a gun or club or knife
To take another monkey's life
Yes, Man descended the ornery cuss
But brothers, he didn't descend from us!

Evolution – The Monkey's Viewpoint Anon

CHAPTER 19

To attain knowledge, add something every day
To attain wisdom, remove something every day

Lao-Tzu, Chinese philosopher

Let us now catch up on my own work again for like Bilbo Baggins in that lovely quote from *Lord of the Rings "The road goes ever on and on."*

Just before Christmas 2011 a client asked my opinion on a therapy called Hellerwork. I had heard about it but that was all. Investigation now showed that it had good vibrations and was appropriate for helping people at the present time. I have regularly noticed that as some doors close others will always open, and this treatment did indeed seem to be very interesting. There are currently only five practitioners in the country using this therapy, although it has been around for some time. Very quickly I found one person after another needed it, so it was obviously going to require my "Thought" processes. So, what is Hellerwork?

Well, to quote from the handbook *Bodywise* by Joseph Heller and William A. Henkin, *"it makes the connection between life issues and natural body alignment and shows how to restore the body's natural balance from the inside out and how a person can regain control and become a full time owner of the body."* I certainly like that; it sits very comfortably with all my understanding of life. Over the past two years I had been greatly involved in unhappiness and suffering so this technique appeared to be the next move on. With Hellerwork, one could say that all the "hands on" therapies seem to come into one. Initially it was needed by everyone and has become part of the healing process. Then Sound therapy began to arise through the Solfeggio tones already described in Chapter 16. A completely new healing mode may be emerging, and I'm reminded of the words given to me 20 years ago about being involved with the northern colony of Atlantis that birthed the sound systems.

Furthermore, as human beings begin to see some light at the end of the tunnel and reach a more balanced state of harmony the focus may move to the animal world. Recently, right out of the blue, I suddenly noticed all the animals were "shut down" energetically. This had never happened before. After three days, contact came back, but for the first time they have needed "collective work" for the release of unhappiness and sorrow with lavender colour healing followed by one of the Solfeggio sound frequencies which is linked to "undoing situations and facilitating change!" They may simply have had enough! This also shows that it could be timely for human beings to begin to stop projecting human unhappiness on to animals. Animals also need regular rebalancing of the Ph acid and alkaline in their bodies as has been the case for us humans. If we consider that a small, more evolved number of people are here as "the Family of Light" encoded to help wake up the rest of the planetary souls, it may also be the same in the case of the animal world. Domesticated animals very close to their owners may also play a huge role in a similar way with other animals. These same "evolved animals" may also help release the suffering of those animals bred for the food industry and for medical experimentation.

As this journey proceeds, and more and more people are released from pain and suffering, so healing takes different directions and seems to speed up.

I happened to talk to a client who mentioned something called "Universal Calibration Lattice" that recalibrates our Light Body which is part of our multidimensional unseen body. Almost immediately it was needed by everyone collectively. This process is helping us to realign with the fifth dimension energy now on the planet. A very short time later I learnt about a "Dolphin Brain Repatterning" that can heal the nervous system and repattern the brain. So, surprise, surprise, everyone now needed this on a collective and sometimes individual level too. We shall see how important it has been for my work to incorporate healing at this collective level. From the book *The Creator Speaks* channelled by Michelle Phillips in 2004, but not published until 2009, which I delve into in a deeper way later on, we learn how timely it is to return from the duality existent in the world back into oneness. The "collective" is a bit like a flock of sheep calling the lost sheep back into the fold from where we have strayed for millions of years.

Following on from the "Dolphin Brain Repatterning", I was speaking to a client about the ancient Japanese art of acupressure called Jin Shin Jyutsu that she practices. I saw it had a positive vibration, another new "tool" for our changing bodies, and this technique is proving a very timely way to release residual emotional pain both individually and collectively.

I say "new tools", although some of them are a rediscovery of ancient knowledge or practices such as the Japanese Acupressure, or "the Flower of Life", as described in the book *The Ancient Secret of the Flower of Life* published in 2000 and written by Drunvalo Melchizedek. What he calls the "Flower of Life" is the *"primary geometric generator of all physical form... the genesis of our entire third dimensional existence... The energy field of evolved humans can be recreated which is the key to "Ascension and the next dimensional world."* Doesn't that sound exciting? Melchizedek describes practices that he found appropriate at the time but I can do this, as everything else, by Thought.

The very latest technique needed is, in comparison, a quiet indulgence for everyone via the Dr Hauschka treatment, bringing harmony to the body using high vibrational products. It can be given, obviously, as a therapy, but again by me collectively and individually by thought. It is always followed by light green colour healing associated with harmony.

The very next day following my discovery of the Dr Hauschka treatment, everybody's energy fields closed down for about four hours. As mentioned previously, this had happened to the animal world, but in the case of us humans, I felt it was very significant as this hadn't occurred for at least 10 years. This temporary shut down was followed by homeopathic remedies at very high potencies and Pre-Conception Point healing, which goes back to stages when everything was pure potential energy! In fact, we were preparing for a very important astrological configuration.

This astrological event was known as the "Transit of Venus", when the planet Venus crosses the Sun. This has only happened six times in recorded history. Prior to the transit (which took place on the 6th June 2012) clients needed the Metamorphic Technique so often that it had to be done by thought. The Metamorphic Technique, as previously mentioned, is to release pre-birth/past-life issues. It was as though we were preparing for something special to happen, and indeed it did! Five days after the "Transit of Venus" clients needed red colour healing anything up to 12 times a day for two weeks. Never has there been a need for the red colour, which is associated with the base chakra, in this amount. I felt it was probably due to the rising of what is known as the Kundalini. Saint Germain explains this as being the feminine energy that rises up through all the chakras to balance the male/female polarities. We have to note that the planet Venus symbolises the "feminine" and the Sun symbolises the "masculine". A few days after the Kundalini rising a client rang me to say that she had seen a number of Irises and felt it was a message to phone me! I discovered she knew a lot about Kundalini yoga in its purist form rather than the more "watered down" version in our western world. I found everyone needed this for a number of days which I left to a higher helping hand!

Could this be part of the long awaited return to oneness from duality?

CHAPTER 20

We are most disconnected, fragmented, exposed and frail,
when we are separated from the deep dream, the story of the
earth's mind, the rhythm of its beating heart. It is the landscape
of our deep imagination. When we read about the real Middle-
earth, we feel reconnected with ourselves.

The Real Middle-Earth Magic and Mystery in the Dark Ages
by Brian Bates

As our awareness rises we shall generally be looking for more inner enrichment from life. It is probably very timely for films such as *Lord of the Rings* and, of course, more recently the Harry Potter Saga and Philip Pullman's "Dark Materials" trilogy of books. Their huge success in capturing our imagination is an indication of our ever present need for fantasy, especially in this down-to-earth, secular and scientific age.

In the fascinating book, quoted above, Brian Bates explores the world from AD 0–1000 shedding a completely different light on everything at that time. It seems that this is the period that most inspired Tolkien to write his books.

From 600 BC onwards, immigrants from the European continent came to England (known as "Albion" at the time) in small boats, and all these different groups became known collectively as Celts, speaking languages that have survived today as Welsh, Cornish, Breton, Manx, Scots Gaelic and Irish. At this time there were only two to three million people. They lived in a tribal way led by chieftains who would later be called Kings and Queens. *"They were bonded together by shared rituals and customs linked to calendar festivals. These small communities gradually extended across North West Europe and Scandinavia. Dialects, details of costume and shared stories of heroic figures were important to their identity."* Their landscape was of trees, streams and hills and they lived in round homes made of wattle and daub with thatched roofs. They followed a self-sufficient style of life based on farming, hunting and weaving. Their culture was simple, and although conditions could be harsh, they had healthy, albeit short, lives. England was known to be rich in natural resources and to have a temperate climate.

Although there was often warfare between the different groups, it was certainly not the Dark Ages recorded by early historians who described these people as primitive barbarians!

We know much from texts written in Latin by the Romans who came after the Celts and invaded England twice, first in 55 BC and again in 54 BC. The Romans regarded the indigenous Celtic tribes as being primitive. However, we have a completely different perspective on these people at this time, thanks to the remarkable information recorded by Bede some hundreds of years later. He was known as an academic priest attached to a local monastery at a time when Christianity was spreading.

The people of Middle-Earth (whether Celts, Anglo-Saxons or the Norse) who came later, all had a view of nature which we would nowadays call enchanted. They sensed a palpable energy we know as "Life Force" and had a spiritual perspective of the whole environment around them. They felt supernatural presences associated with water wells, plants and the galaxies believing that the cosmos was held together by an interlaced web of gold thread visible to wizards.

Their skull size measurements show that their brain capacity was much the same as ours. The women were almost as tall as the men with fair or reddish hair. They loved ornamentation such as gold bracelets and necklaces. The Roman records talked about the famous Celtic warrior Queen Boudica, when, in 61 AD, she led an uprising against the brutality of the Roman overlords.

Roman Britain lasted about 400 years, a sufficiently long period to have a lasting influence in terms of lifestyle and culture. The trading links with Rome also contributed to prosperity, but the price to pay for this period of "modernisation" was the loss of the ancient magic of Middle-Earth which started its decline in the second half of the 1st century AD as imported Christianity saw missionaries fighting to replace ancient spiritual practices.

After the Romans finally left, in AD 450, due to their collapsing rule in other territories and trouble at home, there was an obvious power vacuum and fighting occurred again. Tribal people known as the Picts raided the northern coasts of Britain followed on by the Saxons who were the next largest group of invaders. They were considered to have highborn tribal leaders that came from either Denmark, called the Jutes, or, as some records suggest, the Franks from Germany. Their first leader to gain prominence was Vortigern. Again there was some subjugation of the Celts as had previously happened under the Romans. However, by the end of the 6th century, larger kingdoms emerged which were to evolve into our present-day counties and shires. Alfred the Great emerged as the first leader to cope with the forthcoming invasion of the Norse or Vikings.

By the end of this period the great Anglo Saxon poem "Beowulf" was written down. It tells how in his youth Beowulf achieved glory by fighting and killing a monster called Grendel who had been terrorising people. There has been much debate as to the origins of the poem, a literary work, or a transcription of ancient oral tales. The epic poem is a mixture of historical events and imagination. Tolkein, in his scholarly work, knew the poem very well and was the first to point out the purely literary quality of the text. We can trace the influence of Beowulf in his tales of Bilbo the Hobbit.

With the Norse invaders there was a resurgence of the magical beliefs of Middle-Earth, for the Scandinavians had not yet been subjected to the influence of Christianity. Their languages today have become Danish, Swedish and Norwegian. However, Christianity was spreading to be officially accepted by the Anglo Saxon royal houses and on down to the people. Priests were instructed to promote Christianity and obliterate any trace of "heathenism"!

By the end of the 11th century social, political and religious upheaval throughout Europe had changed official belief and replaced the ancient traditions. In 1066, when William of Normandy came to England to fight Harold for the kingship at the famous battle of Hastings, this is considered to be when a stricter religious epoch arrived alongside a new lot of rulers. The old ways were outlawed and the magical culture of Middle-Earth gave way to the start of the Middle Ages and onwards to this more secular scientific age.

CHAPTER 21

...As the Cherokee say we have all the colours of humanity within us, the white of our bones, the yellow of our marrow, the red of our flesh and the black of our pupils. The same soft skin covers our bones, the same warm blood beats in our hearts. We are all part of the great mystery that is creation...

The Mystery of the Crystal Skulls
by Chris Morton and Ceri Louise Thomas

From the above book we can delve even deeper to discover the very beginnings of our ancient history.

The reader may be somewhat taken aback to pass from historical periods that are the subject of ongoing scholarly research into other types of research that are based on less conventional sources. On entering the realm of "alternative" information, the question of confidence in the author is central and it is therefore an appropriate moment to mention how I decide to include these types of sources such as the book quoted above. In this age of internet, we have access to so much information that we can usually find articles "for" or "against" any controversial subject and we might well think "this is just an opinion". This is, of course, the case, but the way I arrive at my "opinion" is linked to all the rest of the work I do.

As I have already indicated, the healing work I do is only possible if I can connect vibrationally with a client through their name. Everything in the world of matter is energy, and energy has a frequency which, for practical understanding, can be classed as positive, negative, or neutral. When I pick up a positive vibration in people this indicates that they have an inner awareness of themselves in particular, and of life in general. Where people are concerned, one cannot separate them from their activities, for example the author from the book, the composer from the music, or institutions from those involved within them.

At present, around 75 percent of people are not yet "awake" and would come into a neutral vibrational category. According to my experience, a negative vibration usually corresponds to certain "man-made" products, such as drugs, and as such would be toxic. (Of course not all drugs are negative, and some can vibrate as being neutral. We could consider that they are not harmful, but are not useful either! I have not yet come across a conventional drug that vibrates positively!)

The authors I have chosen, and therefore the information they write about, are all people with a high positive vibration which indicates that we can expect their work to have high truth content.

Let us return to the subject of this chapter.

The tribal peoples have remained silent for hundreds of years following the invasion of their territories. Now it is timely for them to share their knowledge with us again.

A very long time ago, at the end of a time they called the Third World of Water, before the continental drift, when the entire world was one continent known as Turtle Island, extraterrestrials arrived from the Pleiades Orion and Sirius looking for a new home. They came to Earth bringing with them the crystal skulls that contained *"all the knowledge of their culture, their maths, science, astronomy and philosophy alongside all their hopes and dreams."* This was to be the template for us as a new species. At this time, the people were not homo sapiens as we know ourselves today, but were known as Neanderthals, or Earth people. It was a golden age when the animals and the people could communicate with each other harmoniously but, as evolvement progressed, our brains grew bigger and bigger due to all the stored genetic memories. This eventually led to birthing difficulties and survival was threatened. The planet Earth went into a period of crisis. We each have two lines of ancestry and genetic memory, Earth memories and those of our celestial ancestors. Silicon was introduced into our genetic memory by the extraterrestrials, so we now contain part of the whole crystalline matrix that links us to the galaxy. Some scientists are becoming aware of this.

Returning again to the book *Bringers of the Dawn*, it was their Pleiadian ancestors who were the original planners of Earth, working with the aspect of consciousness called Light which they remind us is information. It was considered that Earth would be a sharing of information with other galaxies through stored frequencies and through the genetic process.

All of this happened many millions of years ago. Even Lemuria and Atlantis are considered modern in this context, but we know that 500 thousand years ago, there were highly evolved civilisations that are now buried under the ice cap in the southern continent of Australia. Since the beginning of creation, multitudes of cultures and societies have been on and off our planet. Throughout our long, long history, most of the extraterrestrials have been for our upliftment, but apparently some came for other reasons! At a later phase of evolvement there has been conflict over us being the "Living Library" and for 300 thousand years much destruction has taken place and our DNA has been disassembled from the magnificent 12 strands. We have thus moved through many different ages while seeding and planting and cultivating the potentiality of life into the third dimension.

Now, the Pleiadians have started once again to make contact with our planet to help bring everything to its rightful completion. Of course this is still only an option, an opportunity because of the "free will" nature that exists here. In their words we are now coming into an age of Light, a time to reawaken, to a realisation of the Godhead within us and our connectedness with what can be called the Prime Creator/Source of all that Is. Our original destiny as the Family of Light. However, we cannot birth a new consciousness for the future anchored in our experience of the past. We shall need commitment, determination and willpower. The whole universe is based on the "domino effect": that means that everything we do affects everything else around us. We now have to give ourselves "permission to feel", for feeling connects us to Light, and when enough people get to this stage we will create a new planet.

All the healing work I am doing for people reawakens everyone to the original 12 strands of DNA.

CHAPTER 22

As the higher stages of consciousness emerge and develop
they themselves include the basic components of the earlier
world view then add their own new and more differentiated
perceptions. They transcend and include, because they are
more inclusive, more adequate...

A Brief History of Everything by Ken Wilber

Perhaps we should explore other very reliable and timely information coming through to our dimension now to explain that by 1987 the Earth's crystal grid system, sustaining both our human bodies and the planet Earth, was almost dormant, due to our "fall from grace" at the time of the aforementioned planet Lemuria when a schism occurred between humanity and what is known as the Devic Kingdom. Various strata of existences inhabit the universe, some vibrationally higher than Earth, some lower. Cooperation has been necessary in order to maintain a healthy state on the Earth and within ourselves.

The crystal grid system worked perfectly well until the time of Lemuria when we, as an early race of human beings, began to see all matter as inanimate, to use and abuse for the gratification of our senses. Sexuality was unbridled. Illness and disease was the outcome not helped by aberrant weather patterns. Prior to our "fall from grace", record keeping crystals were placed in the crystal grid system which functions like our DNA. At this stage, it was decided that the Devic kingdom would take Lemuria beneath the Pacific Ocean for purification. The record keeping crystals that contained coding for the Divine Plan for humanity and the Earth were removed and placed in a large monolith for safekeeping until we awakened enough to reverse the "fall from grace". As Lemuria sank, the land mass that became Australia and New Zealand was pushed south and the monolith was stored at Ayers Rock. A contingency plan was put in place to help survivors on Earth reverse the effects of the fall. A new record keeper was encoded and placed in the grid system of Atlantis, but this failed too, and Atlantis also went under the Atlantic Ocean for purification. More crystals were placed in Stone Mountain in Atlanta, Georgia; however, since us human beings and our negative energy had caused the downfall of Lemuria and Atlantis we alone were responsible for reactivating the crystals.

Nearer to us on the recorded time scale the consciousness of indigenous tribal people such as the Hopi, Sioux and Mayans contributed to holding the light in their prophecies until 1987 when what we have come to know as the Harmonic Convergence took place. A spiritual initiation for humanity was triggered through Light Workers and the light flowed again as Earth began her "ascension". In 1992 at the first Earth Summit in Rio de Janeiro, 40,000 people were committed to planetary healing, along with many others around the world. Through Divine Grace, we and the Devic kingdom were forgiven for the pain and suffering that we had inflicted on each other. A new covenant of trust and cooperation was established that could enable the healing of both our human bodies and that of Mother Earth.

The Olympic Games in Atlanta, Georgia, in 2000, was an event that would draw humanity's attention in enormous numbers. Light workers gathered there and evoked the Light of God in order to activate the crystals in Stone Mountain. The Devic kingdom and Divinity redistributed the crystals through the Earth's crystal grid and the sacred knowledge flowed into the emotional and mental strata of Earth and into the hearts and minds of humanity, accelerating awakening.

In November 2003 a "critical mass" was reached that would allow the feminine aspect of Divinity to expand love as the comforter. Two powerful solar eclipses occurred at this time and Light Workers would unite with Divine energy creating a Harmonic Concordance which would trigger Earth's ascension into the 5th dimension!

On the special day of 11/11/11, Light Workers went to New Zealand and linked up with the Devic kingdom for the ultimate healing to take place between humanity and the elemental world.

Before our planet could ascend to the fifth dimension much purging would have to take place. Due to the new cooperation, the inclement weather patterns would not cause the disasters that might have been our fate.

In the Year 2012, there would be solar flares and explosions of light from the Sun to enhance Earths transformation into a new Solar Reality.

Wow! What a journey for humanity!

CHAPTER 23

*We are each other's love, flow, inspiration and strength, we are
inseparable, we are one Twin Flame Soul's song*
                              The Creator Speaks by Michelle Phillips

Coming back again to the above book, it was very timely in year 2012 to
explore the deeper meaning of Twin Flames that Michelle Phillips explains
is complete unity and integration from fragmentation. Due to what we know
as the law of Karma, cause/effect that has operated on the planet as part of
our evolution, there has always been duality as seen so powerfully in male/
female energy. At the end of this era, we learn that our full potential cannot
be gained until we return to the healed state of oneness. We were waiting
to see whether the Karmic cause/effect would be spontaneously released at
the end of the year, freeing human beings to grow through interaction with
like-minded others. Up until now, relationships have often been a sort of
bondage not helped by the "till death us do part" inherent in the religious
marriage ceremony. Many years ago I read from *The Aquarian Gospel of
Jesus the Christ* by Levi,

> *"Now marriage in the "sight of law" is but a promise made
> by man and woman by the sanction of a priest to live for "aye
> in harmony and love." No priest, no officer has power from
> God to bind two souls in wedded love...whom God has joined
> together Man cannot part, whom Man has joined together live
> in Sin"*

As we prepare for more freedom in relationships we need to understand the whole nature of communication. My Spiritual Master, in *The Path of Unfoldment,* explains how we are all individualised aspects of the Universal Mind and through the evolving journey over many lifetimes, unresolved issues come through with us collecting as vibrational impressions that make up the subconscious mind and cloud all our conscious thinking. This can be known as our "muddy pot" that has to be refined. Saint Germain, in the book *Twin Souls and Soul Mates*, reminds us of the work that we have to do on ourselves as a starting point before we can meaningfully communicate with others. "Correct meditation" practices, as I mention in my first book, help to refine this "muddy pot". (On this subject, *The Source* by Ursula James, published in 2012, can be a very helpful workbook using the phases of the moon.)

In the Pleiadian teachings there also comes a reminder of "man know thyself". We are just at the beginning of learning to communicate on a meaningful level although, as I constantly remind people, we have all the time in the world now!

Perhaps I can mention here again the thread of my own "silent relationship" that has been weaving in and out of my life for many, many years. Hopefully, not many people will have to experience the traumatic situation that occurred for me in the spring of 2011 when I discovered his obituary a few minutes before I was to take part in a musical event!

In the work I do, I am very used to the necessary changes that take place as the soul prepares to leave this dimension. Anyone having had healing with me usually goes straight to needing blue colour healing, an indication of not having fully expressed themselves while in this dimension. This is followed by many sessions of lavender for grief over missed opportunities. Eventually, they go to needing pink colour healing for love and can at that stage move into the Higher realms. However, concerning this particular person, nothing of the sort happened. In fact, the thought of "Walk-ins" crossed my mind. This is a transitional situation where a soul enters into another body of a living person! Much information exists on the phenomenon and I had read about it many years before, but until now wasn't sure whether I believed that it could happen or not. It seems that it can be an "arrangement" between souls. Something like this was an obvious possibility and as time has gone on, personal experiences seemed to have confirmed it for he has continued to need all the same healing as everyone else and much more! From all accounts, there is a measure of "unfinished business" and it doesn't take much imagination to understand the great difficulties in a situation like this!

Michelle Phillips devotes a whole chapter on the subject in *The Creator Speaks* explaining that perfected soul relationships are required to be on the planet, in incarnation, at this significant time to enable our world to be healed. And, as we shall learn later, this was also to happen to others.

CHAPTER 24

Sexuality is the means of expressing and experiencing harmony and reunion. You do this by first experiencing separation because only through contrast may you know what reunion is
Twin Souls and Soulmates by Saint Germain

We have relationships within every facet of life, so perhaps we can now explore, in a deeper way, the intimate nature of sexuality.

From a lovely book I read a number of years ago, *Rhythms of Vision* by Laurence Blair:

"In the scales of created evolution we can either resist the interchange of energies, or else we can surrender to them and be lifted high in the wind thermals of change, each discovering for themselves more of the immense harmonic geography of the inner world of which our century is standing on the threshold."

Evolution has moved through the ages of female and then male domination, to finally come to understand the need for a complementary approach. It has not often been recognised that everything has to be expressed from inside to out. At this time of rising consciousness, it is urgent for this to be addressed. We learn from Saint Germain that life itself is expressed in maleness and femaleness and seeks to merge itself through the opposite polarities in the genders of male and female as experienced in our physical world. We need to keep reminding ourselves of his words:

"what is relationship but a relationship with SELF...your history, your culture and humanity for eons has sought to separate spirituality from sexuality, to separate God essence/ Divinity with SELF from the physical Self called sexuality. This has caused pain, heartache and heartbreak for unless the Divine SELF is expressed in physical sexuality it is not complete. The whole temple of the body male or female is feminine in essence. The planet is feminine hence the "mother" Earth and the Sun masculine. Throughout the ages there has been much misunderstanding between the sexes, much suspicion experienced around the feminine for it suggests void, darkness, the deep mysterious place of new life. True femininity is intuition and knowingness without explanation."

Much inner emptiness exists, for we are searching for the other part of SELF that can only be discovered through a soul essence merging with the other gender, not only physically, but emotionally and mentally. In this way, we reunite with the Source, the God essence within. We shall come to understand that the heart connection is essential in leading to harmony. True harmony cannot be experienced until we have inner alignment with the source of our own Being. All union is an intermingling of energies and much "diseasement" can be felt if there is no heart connection, for we are actually affected by the soul essence memory of the other person. My spiritual master talked about how all promiscuity is the search for the missing inner connection.

What we know as orgasm is rather like the flow of electricity through the positive and negative charge that brings illumination. When two essences of the polarities come together in physicality it can bring an explosion of orgasmic understanding when passion is recognized in a cosmic sense as being harmonic balance. This creates joy, the ecstasy of Source, exhibited through the creation of all life. We come to realize that at the higher level we are exchanging self with SELF. We find true self empowerment, sovereignty and recognise that we are having a relationship with all of life. At this stage Saint Germain explains that physical exchanges can be wonderful and

Divine, but it is not something that always has to Be, for Divine essence within all nature is a powerful mirror, the dew upon the leaves, the rising waves of the ocean, a sunrise. Kahlil Gibran expresses beauty in a profound way in his book *The Prophet*, one of the very first books I read that had such a deep effect on me.

> *Beauty is not a need but an ecstasy*
> *It is not a mouth thirsting nor an empty hand stretched forth*
> *But rather a heart enflamed and a soul enchanted...*
> *A garden for ever in bloom and a flock of angels forever in*
>   *flight*
> *Beauty is life when life unveils her holy face*
> *But you are life and you are the veil*
> *Beauty is eternity gazing at itself in a mirror*
> *But you are eternity and you are the mirror.*

As we rise in frequency we shall experience further inner unfolding and knowingness leading to alignment which will bring us real joy and happiness. The great mythologist Joseph Campbell had a saying: "follow your bliss". The Pleiadians exhort us to give ourselves permission to feel, feel, feel and find something to be passionate about. Rising to these higher levels *"we shall have a harmonious experience upon the earth plane as God/man to unite physically with another soul essence called Soul mate."* At this stage we will *"draw this situation to us magnetically and electro-magnetically for this is accorded to us when we are not searching outwardly and are unfolding inwardly into further unlimitness."*

From the book *The Creator Speaks*, we learn that soulmates are people we may have known from other lifetimes and with whom we can communicate on a meaningful level. They will mirror back to us aspects of ourselves to bring balance to the male and female within. Seeing and recognising ourselves as love in a conscious way means we will then be ready to go on to draw the Twin flame/Divine blueprint back to us. Until the time that we are ready for this final unity, it may cross our path, but only as a "quickening".

I am talking to more and more clients who would seem to have had this experience and it is obviously difficult for them to come to terms with it. When the timing is right, communication will be very easy as our colour/sound frequency comes together in beautiful harmony. Saint Germain describes this relationship as the *"identical vibration you emit in your personality"* and the rising of the Kundalini energy in 2012 would seem to be such a timely prelude on our journey towards reunion.

We are here at this time to co-create "heaven on earth" and to assist the balancing of all consciousness, for this level of unity *"can permeate the collective karmic structure into its higher form. It can awaken and heal our world as we come into full consciousness"*.

INTERLUDE

I have a little shadow that goes in and out with me,
And what can be the use of him is more than I can see.
He is very, very like me from the heels up to the head;
And I see him jump before me, when I jump into my bed.

The funniest thing about him is the way he likes to grow –
Not at all like proper children, which is always very slow;
For he sometimes shoots up taller like an india-rubber ball,
And he sometimes gets so little that there's none of him at all.

One morning, very early, before the sun was up,
I rose and found the shining dew on every buttercup
But my lazy little shadow, like an arrant sleepy-head,
Had stayed at home behind me and was fast asleep in bed.

My Shadow Robert Louis Stevenson - Poet

CHAPTER 25

... Everything happens <u>for</u> me not <u>to</u> me...
Loving what Is Byron Katie with Stephen Mitchell

Ever since the Venus Transit event at the beginning of June 2012, I've recognised an even greater urgency to release any blockages on the journey back into "oneness." I am certainly doing all I can to help this happen, and I think it may be interesting to give some idea of what this work involves on a daily basis.

Everyday I start early in the morning with what I call Stage 1 of the "collective" healing by thought". I look at all my clients, unless they are temporarily closed down, for example, due to any inappropriate therapy session. This healing session is an ongoing process which constantly evolves as it is regularly "updated" to coin a modern term!

At this time in 2012, everyone who came to me received regeneration, Liquid manna (which contains white powder gold,) a specialised form of vitamin B12 called Methylcobalamin, strontium (for bones) Solfeggio tone(s), U.C.L. (for recalibration of the Light Body), Flower of Life (code of creation), pink colour healing and Azeztulite (described later). This was a very predictable programme for some time and I felt it helped to keep the physical body very strong as we continued to need release of emotional pain, which I am understanding more and more to be the root cause of all health problems, especially any form of physical pain. Just how strong our physical bodies can be, was brought home to me when a client walked into a tram! She fractured her skull along with other injuries but surprised everyone by leaving hospital after just a short stay!

After meditation and breakfast I begin to look at the people needing daily individual help. For example, this can be clients with severe health problems where I correct irregularities in the brain, body or glandular system. Many of these conditions are usually not understood by orthodox practitioners, such as the symptom known as cystic fibrosis. I had a client who had lost his voice, a young girl with grey hair, a woman associated with the taking of the drug thalidomide and people with all sorts of lumps and bumps. Elderly people need a lot of support since their corrected irregularities have caused a longer series of knock-on effects.

This is a completely new phase in the history of humanity and, as the Pleiadians remind us, we cannot call on any past experience to help us understand the symptoms that will occur during this transition, such as excruciating pain that may come and go, or move around the body. Some people can experience heart palpitations, digestive upsets, sleep disturbance patterns and, of course, excessive tiredness.

A client sent me an article in a daily newspaper reporting on a conference arranged by The World Health Organisation alerting medics to a pending crisis as antibiotics are no longer working in an effective way. Of course this doesn't really come as a surprise for me, since antibiotics were developed to address infections that have now moved to the causal level! I had clients presenting a great variety of symptoms from high temperatures, so-called kidney problems, great pain, anger and irritability, etc, etc. They all responded to the release of emotional pain through the Japanese ancient art of acupressure, and, more recently by Jin Shin Jyutsu, given through thought.

Any physical problems in the body can respond well to previously mentioned Hellerwork. Some clients seem hyper-sensitive to sounds in a disorder called tinnitus, or they may see distorted images everywhere which can cause much anxiety. I find strengthening the Light Body with U.C.L. (Universal Calibration Lattice) is helpful as we are moving into the higher frequencies due to a raised level of consciousness.

Throughout the day the collective healing work continues, a bit like a different filling in a sandwich! This is fitted in around 6 to 8 hours of dealing with telephone calls and the work that is subsequently required. I have no computerisation preferring the personal approach. Things are a little quieter over the weekends; however, I always have some hours off during the afternoon to make a break between "shifts" unless I am going out in the evening for singing in my choir during term time.

Towards the end of the day, the more predictable healing comes in again, usually sound healing through Solfeggio tone(s) U.C.L., the Flower of Life, pink colour healing for harmony and then the Azeztulite crystal energy which is described as *"nameless light for high dimensional consciousness and increased vibrational energy"*. It is a vehicle being used by the group of Beings in the higher dimensions known as the Azez to manifest the energy onto Mother Earth. It holds the high vibrational energy of the Great Central Sun. It helps to ground this Spiritual Light into our bodies and energy fields so that great healing can take place. It helps us to recognise ourselves as multi-dimensional Beings of Light. It connects to all the physical transpersonal chakras allowing for blockages of any kind found within the energy fields, or chakras, to be effectively cleared!

So how do I personally fit into all this healing work?

Well, I've seen many therapists, and others in the healing field, neglect themselves which isn't at all helpful for anybody! Looking back, I realise that I have had to undergo very powerful personal healing which began over 20 years ago. I had had ongoing bouts of cystitis (urinary infection) for very many years and later on I also developed cellulitis which is inflammation of any of the tissues of the body. In my case it was in my left leg and was characterised by fever, pain (excruciating for me) and swelling. This particular condition often takes people into hospital, but by this time I had found my way to a homeopath which marked the end of my association with orthodox medicine. (My relationship with this homeopath, which I mention in my earlier book, was to be very important for he encouraged me to pursue my interest in the glandular system.) He supported me through a most difficult time for I had to be off work at the C.A.B. for several weeks, and subsequently had to learn to walk distances again. However, despite the opinions of others around me (typically!), I trusted the body could heal itself and of course it did!

I can now present to all my clients a living example of how perfect health is our birthright and I am certainly number one at the beginning of every day! Or might I say "we" are number one, for these many years of "silent" relationship and integration in this "twin soul" situation seem to have brought us closer and closer towards a reunion of energy. Any necessary healing module needed now is required by both of us. This is the situation that was written about in the book "The Creator Speaks". Furthermore, since the rise of the Kundalini energy, the process may speed up, by resonance, for other people, on the path towards their final reunion with a Twin Flame.

Perhaps in my current, albeit unusual, position we are both now playing a heightened role much like sheep dogs rounding up all the sheep back into the unity of the flock!

Shall we now give our imaginations free flow and learn more about the magical world of former times?

CHAPTER 26

Endeavour, as you look on any physical form to look into that form and to the spirit. See it in the very roots of the trees, in the trunk, branches and leaves. Look always for the spirit behind or within all form.

White Eagle - Spiritual Teacher

Perhaps it would deepen our perspective at this time to learn more about the world of our ancient ancestors.

The practice of Druidry goes back 2000 years and in a fascinating book called *Living Druidry*, Emma Restall Orr explores *"this powerful and ancient spirituality sourced in the sanctity of nature."* It was one of the ancient traditions suppressed by Christianity as it spread absorbing meaningful festivals into the new church Holy days.

Brian Bates. in his book *The Real Middle Earth*. draws on the latest historical and archaeological findings to reconstruct the imaginative world of our past. He visited woodlands, to get an authentic feeling and he describes his experience at Runnymede which is the famous site where King John and high ranking landowners signed the Magna Carta in 1215. Brian Bates says that *"On entering the ancient woodlands the sensation is one of stepping back in time"*. Runnymede is near the banks of the River Thames and in Anglo Saxon times it was known as Rune-Mede, a sacred place for divination. Some of the oaks in the nearby Windsor Park were planted at that time and are still surviving after a thousand years!

Two thousand years ago, at the start of Middle Earth, great woodlands of oak, beech, hornbeam, thorn and ash covered a third of the British Isles, broken up by tracks of open heath and moor land. Trees have always been cut down for the needs of the population, but at that time this was only about one million and therefore the forests could easily re-grow. The Doomsday survey in 1086 showed forest cover was down to about 15 per cent. Today, surveys show deciduous woodland cover in Britain to be as low as 1.5 per cent, with total forest cover of all species of trees reaching about seven per cent of the Island.

Tolkien pays a tribute to this time of ancient forestland with his great wood in *Lord of the Rings* called "Mirkwood" which was, in fact, a real mountainous forest region to the south of Germany. Here in England, many old woodland areas still retain their old names like Wychwood in north-west Oxfordshire.

Trees dominated the lives of the Middle Earth people, always being a template for their imagination. In these times they were not only used for practical purposes or even just appreciated for aesthetic beauty but they were also perceived as having magical powers. As Brian Bates says *"the forests were alive with the chatter of another world"*. Houses were built next to, or even around, trees. Sacred vows such as marriages were carried out in the presence of the spirits of the forest. The tree was believed to form a bridge between the spirits of the Lower world and the Upper world realm of the Gods.

In the "World Tree" of myth Brian Bates talks in particular of the great significance of Yew trees which can be as old as 2,500 years. In fact, many tribal cultures believed that trees are part of a cosmos structured in a way we would term "holographic" with the whole being mirrored in its parts.

According to Norse mythology, the "World Tree" reflects the notion that the heavens whirl about a central beam that pierces earth and sky called "Yggdrasil" or steed, on which the god Odin journeyed to the heavens questing wisdom. The myth describes how Odin climbed into a sacred tree and stayed there for nine days and nights without food. This legend seems to echo the universal experience of Shamans of all cultures and times.

This visionary journey of Odin was to three worlds, the Upperworld, Middle Earth and the Lowerworld. In the Upper realms lived gods and goddesses. Middle Earth around branch and trunk was where human life unfolded. Odin saw these two worlds connected by a rainbow bridge. Deep in the roots of the tree was the third realm, the Underworld which could often be dangerous, but in which one could reap great rewards of wisdom and the parallel that some have made with "Hell" in Christianity is, in fact, a misinterpretation. During Odin's initiation he had a wondrous visionary experience of travelling on the eight legged horse called "Sleipnir". This legend also gives us insight into the way that people of Middle Earth imagined the cosmos.

We may remember that the Runes are also from Scandinavian descent. They are twenty-five little stones *"imprinted with ancient alphabetic script each of whose letters possessed a meaningful name and a signifying sound. Runes were employed for poetry, for inscriptions and for divination yet never evolved as a spoken language."* Ralph Blum, in his lovely little work *The Book of Runes*, explores them as a contemporary oracle. Many times have I dipped into the little velvet bag containing my own stones to pull out a rune for a client, which is always helpful at difficult times.

Continuing deeper into the world of the Middle Earth people we must, of course, remember that their everyday life could be very hard, with many trials such as famine and disease. However, in spite of practical hardship, or maybe because of it, there was also another kind of reality that took them into realms that we might think of now as the land of "fairy stories".

The legendry "Dragon" allowed people very imaginative insights into life's vicissitudes and the natural landscape became an extension of their creative minds. Today, we can actually visit the original location of some of the famous "Dragon lairs". In Mediaeval Christianity, St George was depicted as slaying the dragon, but at this earlier time there was a much deeper meaning of the dragon as being like a snake that could rejuvenate each time it sloughs its skin. It was as if it died to be reborn. Everything was seen as a perpetual cycle, the dragon representing the sentient force behind all life and rebirth. We may link this to the ancient Chinese culture in which the dragon is thought of as the animating principle of every place. For our Middle Earth people it was a fearsome beast, but *"whose presence fired the landscape with magical power that embodied the fate of whole civilisations"*. Legends surround the dragon guarding hoards of treasure as with Tolkien's "Smaug", or Beowulf's dragon. The Anglo Saxons regarded these myths with an *"abiding sense of destiny"*. Concerning the "treasure", gold was considered to be animate and charged with power, and so if they lived in accordance with Mother Earth, they were destined to thrive. It is interesting to notice that the supplement "White Powder Gold" continues today to embody the "elixir of life".

Perhaps we can now begin to get a clearer view of how all this lost understanding was bringing planet Earth to the crisis point in the late 80s when, as explained earlier, the grid system sustaining the Earth was just about dormant due to the schism between us and what is known as the Devic kingdom.

In a book I read many years ago called *Light from Silver Birch* an Indian spirit used to transmit truths to a group of people in the 80s. He described the Devic realm as part of the Elemental life that concerns fairies and similar beings that we probably know as gnomes, brownies and pixies. They all have a part to play in nature's growth since evolution from the lower to the higher is part of the natural law of all life.

We find a similar idea in the book *Bridges* by Aart Jurriaanse who describes the Elementals as being the essence or primordial phase of all creation in both our Solar System and the Universe.

> *"It is through cooperation between all parts of the universe that creates peace, orderliness and harmony which is the ultimate purpose of evolution".*

Having talked of trees and dragons, water was also an important element that captured the imagination of our Middle Earth ancestors. In our times, we are more distanced from the sources of our sustenance and we are not "mindful" in our everyday encounters with water, for example. For these early people the liquid element was invested with spirit. Many of the rivers in Western Europe were dedicated as sanctuaries. The spirits of water sources had a strong presence and appearance as they represented the larger awareness we know of as Mother Earth. Many names of rivers today still refer to the goddesses or spirits of the river as with The River Glen in Lincolnshire and also in Northumberland. The Celtic name "Glanos" means clean, holy and beautiful. Archaeological excavations in 1964 at the head of the River Seine in France revealed many pieces of wood carvings. Seine is named from "Seguana" the ancient goddess revered by the Celtic peoples of ancient France. And before leaving the subject, it is interesting to remember that for the Celts, the Romans and later the Anglo Saxons, water wells represented the life force of fertility.

In the time of the real Middle Earth birds were believed to bring important messages from the spirit world to those who could understand them. From the book *Birds, Divine Messengers* by Andrea Wansbury, I have often seen how significant they can be to us in our world today, and clients regularly ask questions about the significance of a particular bird that had "crossed their path".

As we have moved further and further away from the ancient understanding of the world of nature into a situation of commercial and technological domination, we are faced today with big ecological issues in order to re-establish respect for our planet. However, as we have also learned, trust has now been restored between us and the elemental kingdom and there continues to be a general rise in the consciousness of humanity, so we must have faith in a positive future.

Brian Bates uses the word "wyrd" a lot. One of his books *The Way of Wyrd* explores the mysticism of ancient England. The word "wyrd" in Anglo Saxon is the origin of the modern "weird" meaning "strange" or "unexplainable".

He feels that the *"insights from the imaginative world of our past may help us to understand our own place in the world"*.

CHAPTER 27

I want to animate, bring alive, the image of God to people. I want to make his grand dream clear to everyone, so that every living person may feel His aspiration of love. Man can become happy here and now in this life. The children of people on the Earth today will live in His Paradise. I am not alone. You are not alone. And Paradise will appear as a conjoint co-creation.

Co-creation - Anastasia

Let us now do a considerable leap in time from the life of our ancient ancestors to a contemporary story...

The above quote is from one of a series of nine books (nine in numerology means completion) that have sold over ten million copies and have been translated into twenty languages. They tell about a remarkable woman called Anastasia (in Greek the name means "resurrection".) She was discovered living in the Siberian forest by a trader, Vladimir Megré, in 1995.

She was born in 1969 to parents who died before she could walk and was brought up by her grandfather and great grandfather who was 119 years old at that time! She lived without warm clothing, shelter, or cultivated food, surviving on fruit, nuts, berries and mushrooms brought to her by "wild animals" with which she lived in close harmony.

Anastasia is a descendant from people who have been living like this for hundreds of years. She displays astounding knowledge and wisdom and at her request, Megré abandoned his commercial life to bring the story of her more meaningful perception of life to the outside world. I believe that the relationship that developed between them is probable that of 'twin souls'.

They later had a son who has been brought up as she was in the forest and Megré visits them from time to time.

Having just explored the whole issue of relationships in a former chapter and how central this all is to the healing of our fragmented world, we may be interested to discover, in the very first book of the Anastasia series, how she dismisses the modern male/female sexual encounters. In her words:

> *"It is very important when two people join their lives together that they have a spiritual attraction to each other and unfortunately as a rule everything starts with the carnal."*

She goes on to explain how she feels that we have lost touch with nature and its healing power. Her home is surrounded by cedar trees that can live up to 550 years while storing cosmic energy. We are reminded how the forest areas known as the Taiga are very naturally fertile just with the compost of falling leaves. She is passionate about how the technological world has lost touch with our pristine origins and goes on to describe how she believes that a nine-year-old brought up in the natural world has a much more accurate perception of creation. We are again reminded that most of our great thinkers or teachers had periods of solitude, to live as recluses in the forest or desert and not going to some super academy! On a more everyday level, we hear about "dachiks", people who spend time tending a garden at their "dacha" or country home.

She has strong thoughts on modern education:

> *"we should be considering the perspective, does it help, harm or hinder Man's ability to make sense of our essence and purity for we can create a perfect world by the power of thinking"*

This is the law of attraction yet again! My spiritual master always said *"we just have to refine our minds then we can pick up all the knowledge in the universe, for our minds are the universe"*.

She describes the amazing forest school run by the Academician Mikhail Petrovich Shchetinin who is redefining education. Originally, he was a music teacher and had a long distinguished career in experimental education. In 1991 he was honoured with the title "Akademik" by the Russian Academy of Education. At the forest school there are 300 pupils from all over Russia. They take one year to master the whole ten year public school maths syllabus along with studying three foreign languages. The school was designed, built and decorated by students aged seven to seventeen. They neither recruit nor produce prodigies. They simply give children a chance to discover what already lies within them! It now comes under the Russian Ministry of Education; it charges no tuition fees and does not have to advertise for there is a list of 2000 hopefuls for a place.

Vladimir Megré poses questions about the knowledge brought to us through other sources, such as the Bible and Koran. Anastasia comments that *"faith and belief is expressed in our way of life, in our essence and designated purpose, in our corresponding behaviour and relationships to the environment and to our thinking"*.

People in ancient times used the power of the mind rather than the telephone, or other modern devices for communication. Ten thousand years ago, the planet was visited by beings that gradually lost their link to the high intelligence of the universe. This led the Earth getting closer and closer to disaster. However, a few people still possessed high ability and they wanted to preserve it. Those that lived in the part of the world we now know as Russia built chambers to enable universal wisdom to be obtained through meditation within them. These places were more powerful receivers than Egyptian pyramids for which they were a prototype. People at a certain age would enter these places to go into *"eternal meditation"* preceding death. This is how the knowledge has been accessed down the ages by people entering the chambers now known as Dolmens. They were falling into neglect, but due to recent understanding as to their purpose, especially through the books associated with Anastasia, interest has been revived. Anastasia's "foremother" had all this perfect knowledge and the ability to communicate with the mind of the universe. It has been proven that as one approaches the sacred places, the energy level changes. Vladimir Megré in a special visit to these sites has acknowledged their gratitude to the ancient ancestors of Russia.

It is very difficult for our modern world to take in the significance of a person like Anastasia living in our midst and she did have problems when news of her abilities reached "higher levels". However, unbelievable things happened to protect and prevent her capture. As we proceed through the amazing series of books, Anastasia sheds light on how history has been distorted or kept secret for thousands of years and shedding light on the causes of war, oppression and violence in the modern world. She has a vision of the future in which she exposes the extraordinary process by which all armaments will be removed from the planet. She paints images of exquisite beauty, abundance, peace and harmony. When she talks to Megré on the philosophy of life she says:

> *"my son, the universe itself is a thought, a thought from which was born a dream which is partially visible as matter. When you approach the edge of all creation your thought will reveal a new beginning and continuation. From obscurity will come a new and resplendent birth of you and it will reflect in itself your soul, your dreams, your whole aspirations. My son, you are infinite you are eternal. Within you are your dreams of creation!"*

As in *The Creator Speaks*, Anastasia offers an inspirational view of the beginning of creation with the first human living to 118 years before being joined by the first feminine presence. Anastasia calls her the Goddess created from the Divine Dream that can restore the Earth to its resplendent pristine worth. She tells us it is the female who will now transform the whole Earth into the blossoming garden of the Divine Dream.

Anastasia believes that a new Dawn will begin in Russia proving that the spirituality and knowledge inherent in our origins are more significant than technology, for we are *"becoming biological robots not having enough time to contemplate the essence of Being or listen to what another is saying, no time to reflect on our own destiny!"* .

It is interesting to note that the chakra system superimposed across the world places the crown chakra at this time in Russia! Incidentally, the heart chakra is in England!

The ancient history of Russia is perhaps less well known than that of some other cultures. Anastasia is a Vedruss from the Yugra aboriginal group still living in the far north of Siberia. These people, she explains, are lying dormant but have thrived here in Russia, Ukraine, Belarus, England, Germany, France, India, China and many other states large and small. Anastasia describes the Vedic Age in which people reached a level of sensitive knowledge that enabled them to create energetic images through "collective thought". This lasted 9,000 years, but deteriorated due to the loss of "pure thought". This resulted in the Occult Age that lasted for one thousand years and was the beginning of the deterioration that we know today. During the earlier Vedic Age, *"Man did not bow down before God, nor was there the multitude of religions which sprung up afterwards. There was a culture to life. People lived in a Divine way of life... the power of the energy of thought has been neglected in the universe, everything, including ourselves is created by the energy of thought".*

Despite organised campaigns to discredit the forest school, which even involved unexplained fires, Anastasia's dream is beginning to take shape following on from earlier visionaries such as Alexander Chayanov (1888-1937) who back in the 1920's foresaw the eventual return of the country to predominantly rural living after the fall of Communism. He described the Moscow of the future as being a garden city populated mostly by tourists and accurately predicted the rise of the Dacha movement that would dominate the country's agriculture. Chayanov's views were publicly attacked by Stalin at the time and he was executed.

In 2003, three years after the publication of one of the Anastasia books, Russian President Putin signed into federal law the "Private Garden Plot Act" whereby Russian citizens can receive from the state plots of land, free of charge, and ownership becomes private and inheritable. The produce grown on the land is not taxable. Then in 2006 President Putin introduced to the Russian Parliament another law to further facilitate the acquisition of land for gardening. This is perhaps another indication of how Anastasia's vision is becoming reality, for "Dachnik Day" is now celebrated on July 23rd every year by millions of gardeners throughout Russia and beyond.

We hear from a philosophy professor that *"Anastasia's creative potential is a gift of God, a gift of nature which is universal not merely a personal gift to her. All of us collectively and individually are connected to the Cosmos"*.

If people are tempted to relocate themselves in Russia after reading these books, they may first consider her comments!

> *"I have not invited anyone to the taiga. What would you do here? If your intentions are good let them be expressed right there, where you are living. Let your love illuminate those living around you!"*

Having read and re-read this series of books, I quite agree with the remarks made by many people:

> *"If you have to choose just one author to read in your life then this series would be it."*

Even the book covers are an inspiration in themselves. The illustration on the cover of *The New Civilisation* depicts a Nautilus, a mollusc, which she says is a symbol of expansion and renewal and of the great things achieved with patience and commitment under the guidance of Natural Law. I would also like to quote Anastasia's words from the frontispiece of the same book,

> *"Such beneficial energy can flow from Man as has never before been seen. Every living creature on the Earth needs this energy just as it needs air, sunshine and water. And even sunlight is a reflection of the great energy emanating from Man"*.

I think it's appropriate to end this chapter with a summary of the translator's lengthy "after word", at the end of the whole series, which he calls *"A voyage of self-discovery"*.

> *"...The most frequently asked readers' question can be summed up in the opening sentence of a Quebec writer's review of the series. ("Le Journal Vert" spring 2007) "Anastasia existe-t-elle? (Does Anastasia exist?)*
>
> *Some people do dismiss her as a figment of Megré's imagination whereas others see her as the reincarnation of some ancient prophet."*

The translator poses some interesting questions himself.

> *"What does it mean to exist? Is existence an objective or subjective state? Is existence confined to material perception or can it be determined by non-material criteria? (Faith, for example.) Megré quotes Anastasia herself as saying "I exist for those for whom I exist."*

A few other personages have also been subject to questioning over the ages, names like Shakespeare, Santa Claus and even Jesus, but the same reply may be made as that of a devout committed Christian sent a treatise to Leo Tolstoy (his mentor) in 1888 in which he concludes that:

> *"whoever wrote the gospels makes no difference to me. It is the truth imparted, a precious jewel, and my task, (he said), is to know the price and to know why it is so precious".*

The translator of the Anastasia books explains that

> *"the ideas and intricately crafted literary structure are evident throughout the books. If it should somehow turn out that the story of Anastasia was the author's invention then Vladimir Megré would have to be considered to be one of the world's cleverest and most inspirational writers since Shakespeare. What is described must have come from some form of personal experience".*

INTERLUDE

Look upwards
Cloud pictures in the sky
Ever changing
Cannot grasp or
Hold onto
Reflects the pattern
Of life
Just to gaze
At the wonder of creation
An early sunrise
Showers of rain
Blaze of midday sun
Feel the warmth
Be in the moment
Amidst a pageant
That can move through
Gold to azure blue and
Deepest crimson
Moon and stars a
Glittering vista
Timelessness
EVERLASTING

Skyscape Iris Sparkes

CHAPTER 28

Long ago when the world was brand new, before animals or birds, the sun rose into the sky and brought the first day. The flowers jumped up and stared around astonished. Then from every side, from under leaves and from behind rocks, creatures began to appear.

> The Dreamfighter and Other Creation Tales
> Ted Hughes, Poet Laureate 1984

I think it is timely that the animals have a whole chapter to themselves for it is the first time, in my experience, that as a species they have been displaying evidence that suggests a jump in their consciousness. They now seem to be affected vibrationally by human evolvement. It's also the first time that they have needed healing at the "collective" level, as we do.

I first noticed a change in behaviour in March 2012 as they were all "shut down" for a few days. When the vibrations had "resurrected", I found that all the animals needed lavender colour healing for unhappiness, and sound healing through one of the solfeggio tones that is linked to "facilitating change!"

Let's now delve deeper into their world to enjoy hearing stories from people who have made in-depth studies. I was impressed by a book I read some years ago by Bill Schul called *The Psychic Power of Animals*. He describes incredible true accounts about the secret world of animals. We hear about how dogs trace their owners, read minds, and have the ability to think and reason. Lyall Watson, the biologist, explains:

"This is the secret of life. It means that there is a continuous communication not only between living things and their environment but amongst all living things in that environment. An intricate web of interaction connects all life into one vast self-interacting system. Each part is related to every other part and we are all part of the whole."

An animal communicator joins the regular group of people who meet at my house on a monthly basis. She has many years of work experience and confirms how communication with animals plays such an important part in understanding them. Bill Schul describes how a horse was being treated for lameness in the hind quarters. The condition was getting worse despite the efforts of several excellent vets. In desperation, the owner asked a communicator to find out what was wrong with him. *"I backed into a rough beam in my stable and drove a splinter into my spinal column"* the horse informed the communicator who was also psychic. He explained that communication takes place on the level of mental images. Verbal exchange is not necessary, for it is seen in the mind and interpreted. The owner informed the vet and close examination revealed this to be the case. The splinter was removed and the horse got well!

In the opinion of people who work a lot with dogs, the little ones can be the most insecure and this may account for their nervous temperament. German Shepherds are often thought to be some of the most intelligent, while cats can be more secretive than dogs and so less communicative on the whole.

Perhaps we can well understand how animals reflect, to a large extent, what they see in the people around them. We hear about a hamster that was very quiet on his wheel, due to the owner not liking noise around her! Not to mention the Doberman who was considered to be dangerous. In fact, he was very lonely and desperate for loving attention, despising the image he gave of himself. He responded eagerly to a friendly approach that completely changed his behaviour.

There have been many well-known stories of how humans forge great links with animals. We remember Monty Roberts, subject of the documentary

"The Real Horse Whisperer", who revolutionised the relationship between a man and a mustang horse considered to be very wild. *Warhorse* is another film about a strong man /horse relationship. There are so many similar stories!

We are probably less familiar with demonstrations of what we could call extrasensory perception referred to as "psi", of Greek origin, used generically for all types of psychic phenomena. Studies have been carried out on gerbils, dogs, hamsters and cats that suggest that the "psi" in animals is apparently not of recent evolution. Bill Schul gives the example of a cat that had lived very closely to his owner for 4 years that became very upset when the owner had to make a trip away. It adjusted, until a month afterwards the cat was found meowing in a corner, refusing to eat and ignoring all attention. Shortly after noon the next day, the cat broke out into loud yowling. Within the hour, a neighbour received a telephone call to say that the cat's owner had died from a heart attack en route to hospital!

Other close observation suggests that animals can have cosmic clocks. Henry was described as a large, gregarious, black cat, but his owner was not disposed towards conversation. Henry was obviously bored and would arrive regularly on a neighbour's doorstep. At a set hour, Henry would continue a social round demanding attention everywhere he went. His visits were always punctual before he returned home to his owner at the end of the day!

This, and other similar stories, attest to the fact that:

> *"that all living organisms exist in the pulsating sea of energies serving as receivers, transformers and projectors. Each human being, animal and plant is related to all other life in the Earth's magnetic field and through it to the changes in the electrical fields of the moon and sun."*

Lyall Watson describes how ocean animals are observed in laboratories close to the sea. In his well known book *Supernature*, he describes how nature becomes so well adapted to its habitat: *"oysters open their shells to feed at high tide and close down to prevent damage and drying out during the ebb of the tide"*. Observation of animal behaviour has often been used to alert humans to danger. The Japanese who live on a fracture line keep gold fish that swim in a frantic way indicating seismic activity. It is, of course, well known how in one of the recent tsunamis, wild animals relocated to higher ground ahead of the event. One explanation could be that animals may be in some ways closer to the Universal Mind because they are not occupied so intently with the activities of the brain! Jamie Sams and David Carson certainly feel that animals can be used as a modern oracle, much like the runes. In their book *Medicine Cards* they give insights into the significance of different animals that "cross our path".

There are fascinating stories of how owls have hooted at bedroom windows when a member, or a very close member, of the family dies and I remember being very affected by a book that I read quite a long time ago on this subject: *I Heard the Owl Call My Name* by Margaret Craven. It relates the story of how a young vicar is sent to British Columbia, home of the Kwakwaka'wakw nation. He doesn't know that in fact he is suffering from a fatal disease and he is sent to this place to learn life's lessons in the time that is left. The title derives from the tribal belief that when one hears the owl call one's name, death is imminent.

Tribal people, of course, have always had great reverence for birds and wild animals. The chief Medicine Man of the Shoshone Indian nation, Rolling Thunder, says:

> *"Medicine Man must learn complete Oneness with all forms of life...he must direct his consciousness to the animal and understand himself as a bird, a coyote and so on. He must actually see through the eyes of the coyote, hear through his ears and think through his thoughts..."*

From the book *Kinship with All Life*, J. Allen Boone tells us about a man, Mojave Dan, who spent his life in the desert having silent two-way conversations with dogs, wild animals, snakes, insects, birds and, indeed, everything that crossed his path. Perhaps snakes are the most underrated and unloved members of the animal kingdom yet, without fins they can swim as fast as most fish, some can climb trees, they sleep without closing their eyes and can detect sound even if they don't have complete ears. Although they crawl across the ground they are the cleanest of animals and are especially revered by American Indians and also in Ancient Greece. The "Coiled Serpent" is the symbol of the Kundalini previously mentioned.

We all know how domesticated animals can become very close to their owners, but Bill Schul tells us about a link between a wild bird and a bird lover, who during his life had a relationship with many wild birds. During his waning years, only one bird remained a song thrush. She refused to fly away and would sometimes perch on his shoulder and head. When the man became very ill, the bird sang very little. On the day the man died the bird didn't sing at all. The coffin had been in the house and as it was taken out of the house by the pall bearers the thrush began to sing her heart out like a requiem. As the hearse left for the cemetery she was silent again for she, too, had died. What a touching story.

I have often mentioned how people can be helped after death, and on looking at the bird lover's name I saw that he had gone straight to Higher realms while this can often take years for many souls.

Perhaps I could mention here how I had quite an amazing little encounter with a wild bird that suddenly seemed to land on the bonnet of my car as I was standing next to it outside my cottage. Although it was a large bird, it seemed to be a young one. It looked at me and tweeted. We kept up a two way "conversation" and as I got nearer and nearer it actually let me stroke it! After a certain time, it flew to the ground and waddled off. Yes, maybe our relationship to the wild creatures is about to change.

A rather humorous story was mentioned to me just ahead of writing this chapter on animals. A pair of tortoises, male and female, had lived in happy companionship for 115 years when suddenly the female fell out with her partner! After 115 years!

Perhaps the most fascinating of stories was recorded about the rapport between Boone and a house fly he called Freddie who made friends with each other. Each morning, Freddie would land on his shaving mirror. Boone would invite him to climb on to his finger and would gently stroke his wings. They would play together and eventually Freddie would come when

Boone called his name! He stresses the need for human beings to recognise *"that real communication and rapport with animals depends largely upon respect for their intelligence and feelings. Without this acceptance animals might be trained to obey human commands but there could be no real sharing"*. Boone is probably best known for his connection to the German shepherd dog, Strongheart, who become a movie celebrity and who taught him so much.

"Telling the bees" is an ancient tradition and we read about how when a beekeeper died, the family went round to tell the news to fourteen of his beehives. As relatives and friends were gathered at his graveside the bees from over a mile away gathered on and about the coffin. They stayed for half-an-hour and then returned to their hives.

We can't forget about dolphins in this chapter. Scientists are discovering that they have a larger cerebral cortex than us and the "grey folded blanket" enveloping the rest of our brain, supposedly providing us with superior reasoning power, is, in fact, more complex in the dolphins than in ourselves! They have been known to give help to humans in danger. They will go to any length to save an injured member of their own kind and are fearless in danger.

Animal's memories are legendary. I was told about a TV news item about two gorillas who met up after not having seen each other for nine years. They actually shook hands and gave each other a hug! We may have heard of the story of the "Harrods Lion" who was reintroduced to the wild after a year-long close relationship with its two owners. They went back a year later and the lion still remembered them in a moving greeting scene.

My spiritual master, in one of his talks, explained how an animal goes to a different dimension before the next stage of their evolution towards the human. Is this the missing link that Darwin couldn't comprehend?

CHAPTER 29

The only person you can depend on for your
happiness is yourself
Teach yourself the I Ching by Andy Baggot

Let's move back again to the more complicated subject of us human beings!

I'm sure that by now, we all realise what an extraordinary time we are living in, for it is probably the first time in our recorded history that it is possible for the human body to make a self-healing journey to perfect health, and hence live as long as we choose. Books like *Bringers of the Dawn* by Barbara Marciniak, remind us that the inhabitants of planet Earth have been in the *"dungeon of time for so long"*, but now we are able to regain our rightful sovereignty through self-empowerment. Rising to a higher level of consciousness, we can understand the causal levels of all health problems. The body can rebalance itself with support at this present stage. People like the descendants of the Ancient Inca, in Peru, have always retained this knowledge and, after visiting there in 1999, I've discovered that it is probably my destiny to translate their knowledge appropriately, through thought healing, in accordance with the recent vibrational changes on planet Earth. This, as explained, is leading to the need for new tools to assist the self-healing process.

In July 2012, the healing journey reached the stage where the new crystal energy of Azez was needed, as explained. This was followed by another new crystal energy called Herderite which awakens dormant areas of the brain. During this time, pre-conception point healing was necessary for two days and later, two-and-a-half days. Pre-conception point healing is described as the *"thinking point, the starting point for the individuals we are to become. It is a time of receiving and understanding, of insight and knowledge".* So we learn how far back this personal evolutionary journey is taking us! No wonder clients are often asking "how long is all this going to take!"

There were three "shut downs" in 2012. The last of them involved humans and animals together. It may have been due to solar flares in the atmosphere that we had been told would happen that year. This situation is always followed by an acceleration of everything after the "shut down". The humans needed a very high potency of the homeopathic remedy, Teraxacum, for repressed anger. The animals all needed the Metamorphic Technique. Yes, it can be for them too! The release of emotional pain continued to be needed until a client mentioned another Japanese therapy called Amatsu, and low and behold, from that moment, no more of the Jin Shin Jyutsu, Japanese acupressure for the release of emotional pain, was needed. It doesn't mean that all the aches and pains have gone, but a particular aspect has been released. Amatsu is an all-embracing therapy and was helpful in the following stage doing some "repair work" since destructive emotions can actually damage the physical body. There was a similar situation in December 2009, when six months of pain release was followed by the cleanser Zeolite for weeks and weeks as a "clean up" preparation for these later stages.

We learn that many other species in the universe do not know about emotions. Much interest is now centred on planet Earth for through feeling, generated by emotion, we connect with our spiritual self! There has to be a *"re-emergence of healthy emotions to bring us into a wholeness and richness of multidimensional Being".* This process is very valuable to the evolution of the whole universe, although at present, we have been described as adolescents in the field of emotions.

The mission of my spiritual master was to open up the heart centre and, through correct meditation practices, release unhealthy emotions from many past lifetime encounters.

At this point, it was very appropriate to learn from a client about a particular healing therapy that played a large part in release of destructive emotions, ancient traumas and fears. This is called Metatronic Healing;

described as an angelic healing gift guided by the energies of Archangel Metatron.

> *"It gently and progressively permeates the heart centre to restore the forgotten matrix, the geometrically perfect template of our original divinely given light nature, so that we can re-establish ourselves as co-creators with Divinity."*

Isn't that a wonderful gift to us all?

Not the end of the journey, however, for a number of people needed homeopathy at the highest MM potencies. Heklalava, associated with traumatic life events such as bullying. Vipera is to do with melancholy, depression, being forsaken and/or burdened with past life memories and heavy ancestral Karma. Lilium Tigrinum is associated with sexual issues. Staphysagria, to do with buried anger and resentment. Cactus Grandiflorus helps to deal with desolation, feeling imprisoned by the world and longing for freedom.

Trager therapy crossed my path at this time for clients, too. It helps release habitual patterning.

From the middle of November 2012, something called Bulgarian Rose Otto was needed collectively. It is a flower remedy, and as the name suggests it is all about love. We shall see it was preparing humanity for opening up the heart centre. Initially, it was preceded by Lavender colour healing releasing residual unhappiness, followed by Zeolite that cleanses everything that unhappiness releases. All this seemed so timely, for we were approaching some very important dates. The lunar eclipse on November 28th, we discover, was indeed about opening up the heart centre to pave the way for the important December events.

On the 12th of December, we learnt that the greatest influx of Divine Love that humanity has ever experienced was centred on planet Earth. I confirmed this by picking up the need for pink colour healing collectively three times during the day. Each time it was needed for eleven minutes. Eleven, of course, is a master number in the universe. It was hardly surprising that one of the "shut downs" of energy occurred during this day.

The day ended with the collective need for the supplement white powder gold, associated with optimum health. At my cottage, we had a special gathering of people that day. Meditation began at 12.12 and was preceded by some lovely music sung by a friar from Assisi; "Make me a Channel of Your Peace". After meditation we listened to the song "Somewhere over the Rainbow". One of the members of our group brought along a large bunch of pink roses and everybody was given one to take home.

From the 12th to the 21st December 2012, there was a daily, collective need for Bulgarian Rose Otto; sometimes for eleven minutes, and sometimes eleven times a day!

So, 21st December 2012 wasn't the end of the world! However, it was the birthing of a new *"Renaissance of Divine Love through the thoughts, words, feelings, actions and beliefs abiding on Earth, for Earth will align with the Galactic Core of the Milky Way"*.

Yes, as I learnt over these three years, a closed heart centre has resulted in much suffering that has wreaked havoc in the bodies of so many people. The release of layer-upon-layer of the build up that had taken place over hundreds of lifetimes, is an ongoing process before our love centre can shine through to bring us inner joy.

Following the days after 21st December, pink colour healing was sometimes needed for twenty-two times a day! (another master number).

I could hardly believe it when on New Year's Eve everybody needed the homeopathic remedy Platinum Metallicum for eleven minutes again! This remedy is to do with Cosmic Alignment. Wow! So, on we go into a New Age.

CHAPTER 30

For I dipped into the future
Far as the eye could see
Saw the vision of the world and
All the wonder that would be

Alfred Lord Tennyson - Poet

This was the vision of Tennyson, poet Laureate from 1850–1892. So, there have always been those that knew a happier world was our destiny.

As we finally leave behind this suffering age, what happened in the early months of 2013?

At the close of 2012, the Rose Otto and the pink colour healing associated with divine love continued to very important. However, the Metamorphic Technique associated with pre-birth/past lives was no longer needed.

As has already been said, this is the biggest transition ever experienced by humanity and time is required to adjust to it all. It is even difficult to imagine that we can, at last, experience love and joy.

Much sound healing through Solfeggio tone frequencies was necessary. Sometimes it was the whole Solfeggio scale, but particularly the frequency for "connection/relationships". In this case, the "connection/relationships" were on an inner rather than an outer level. Much residual release of deep blockages within the human race continues, compounded by years of "symptom" treatment which has had the effect of pushing the causes deeper and deeper. Obviously, elderly people have been the most affected, but individual people of all age groups have been carrying deep ancestral memories.

Clients often asked me how they could help themselves at this stage. There is no simple answer as we need to gain deeper and deeper understanding of "self-love". It wasn't by chance that a member of our monthly group brought copies of the newspaper *Positive News* for everyone before Christmas. This is printed four times a year. Right across the centre pages was an article by an award winning filmmaker/musician and "creative catalyst", Jamie Catto, who inspires people to realise their potential. One paragraph in particular caught my eye:

> *"I think we're living in a world where we've all agreed a massive compromise through the pursuit of approval. We get addicted to the "crack" of approval very early on in life. Because of this, we edit ourselves incrementally until we are these 30% versions of ourselves tailored perfectly for the part."*

Relationships are about to undergo much change since the release of Karmic obligation allows complete freedom to undergo positive growth. In my former book *From Caterpillar to Butterfly*, I devote a whole chapter to the nature of different relationships for, as I say, "family" has been the convenient way to deal with unfinished Karmic business. Once this is released, people may begin to drift apart unless they are on the same wavelength. This understanding can be especially helpful to clients who are having difficult family relationships. Although it is often difficult to accept, children born into this situation may, in fact, have more of a natural link to one or the other of the parents. It is also possible that they may have no link with their brothers or sisters.

However, the eventual outcome of the release of Karma will mean that in the future more people will be able to have compatible relationships and happier families will be the norm. As with other old tools, standard counselling, often looking for compromises, now needs to understand the deeper meaning of life.

Times of change are often difficult to adjust to, but the good news is that as the heart centre gradually opens and we *experience* inner love and joy, we shall *know* how to handle situations better. I already had glimpses of this positive change as I was more often able to tell clients that a particular relationship was a special one. Once released from our "baggage" we shall come into a more integrated state and when it is timely, we shall draw more meaningful relationships towards us. These are pleasant reflections as we continue on our journey!

As January progressed, I found Resonance Re-patterning was needed again. This is a "talk therapy" which is able to pick up the life issue blockages that are causing a problem.

I had referred people for this form of healing well over a year before. Now I found it was suddenly needed collectively, four times a day, by thought. Each time Zeolite was needed as a cleanser confirming, yet again, how feelings "gunge up" the internal body. Much lavender colour healing followed, for release of unhappiness. Pink colour healing was also necessary every day, just to remind us of our destiny.

Something quite amazing occurred on St Valentine's Day. For eleven minutes, everybody collectively wanted the homeopathic remedy Lilium Tigrinum at the MM highest potency. This was not only needed for that day, but also for the following two days. Lilium Tigrinum is for repressed desires, especially sexual. Somebody was letting me know that humanity is looking for love in completely the wrong direction; outside instead of within! And as usual, the homeopathy was coupled with pink colour healing for divine love!

There seemed to be an urgency to change our understanding, and indeed this remedy was followed by the other homeopathic remedies: Vipera for doom/gloom, Staphysagria for repressed anger, Heklalava, for a history of traumatic life events. Furthermore, Resonance Re-pattering revealed yet a further eleven blockages which needed to be cleared one after the other in only one day by thought. We must remember that the release of blockages usually has to be done layer by layer, otherwise the process may be too overwhelming. In between each release, the Zeolite cleanser was necessary.

At the end of December 2009, I had noticed that the pineal gland, in the endocrine glandular system, had become spontaneously active. As we came up to the end of 2012, it was then developing a problem causing the energy of the whole system to grow weaker and weaker. By the beginning of 2013, every new person needed the same healing as those with the cellular imbalance of cancer. Everyone also needed red colour healing to revive the root chakra. It was as though the December 2009 reactivation of the gland was now "wilting". I pondered that it could perhaps be revived again through the love vibration, and that is what did happen. Prior to Easter, pink colour healing was needed in large quantities and, low and behold, a little miracle occurred that revived everything. Everyone had therefore played their part as an act of service for the rest of humanity. My spiritual master often reminded us that "everything serves in life; the flower by its scent, the fire through heat." This was, indeed, an amazing demonstration of the power of love.

CHAPTER 31

It's only a tiny rosebud
A flower of God's design...
For the pathway that lies before me
My heavenly Father knows
I'll trust Him to unfold the moments
Just as He unfolds the rose

Anon

After Easter 2013, another ground-breaking event was about to occur. I had always had to realign the spine for all new clients coming to me. The need for this was originally brought to our attention by a Swiss man, R.C. Schümperli, and led to the development of the physical therapy known as AtlasPROfilax to correct this.

Suddenly I noticed it wasn't necessary anymore, and this seemed to be connected to the astronomical event mentioned in a book called *The Coming of the Holy Grail* by Claire Nahmad and Michael Revil, published in 2012. They talk about the fact that a planet known as Planet X, or Nibiru, would come into the orbit of our Earth around the end of 2012 or early 2013, and this would reverse the anti-clockwise spin that our planet had been in for thousands of years. I will mention this book again a bit further on.

Anyway, all I now need to do is to give one of the Solfeggio tones to settle things down in the spine.

Easter was an important time in other ways, for everyone started to need "Cosmic Elements" instead of the usual supplements. I myself had been having these "Cosmic Elements" for a number of months prior to everybody else. Or shall I say "we" had been having these, for in our soul unity, we both automatically need the same thing.

So we can all now begin to think of ourselves as "Cosmic Beings"!

"What next?" I wondered.

It was to be the release of further irregularities in the body, followed by different high homeopathic formulas all associated with the nervous system in one way or another. This was indeed to be very significant, but what followed is thanks to a quite amazing and unique French neurologist, an ear, nose and throat specialist, Professor Alfred Tomatis (1920–2001.) For fifty years, Tomatis explored the connection between our ears and the brain. He revealed how our ears can be *"gateways to actualising one's hidden potential"*.

He discovered that one of the primary functions of the ears is to convert sound waves into electrochemical impulses that "recharge" the brain. Sound that comes through the ears, or by bone conduction, is, in fact, a nutrient that can charge or discharge the nervous system. Apparently 70% of the energy that the brain requires in order to function comes through the ears! Tomatis developed tests to measure how well the ears could "listen" beyond just "hearing". Courses were developed in listening centres all over the world to correct problems that can arise from stress, ear infections, accidents, illness and emotional and physical trauma. I had known about the work of Alfred Tomatis for many years and had always had it "on my list" to consider. So, no surprise that at this point it was timely for everyone. As in the case of all therapies, I just "ask" that it be done by thought. There was a big focus on the Tomatis listening for several weeks until it settled down to being needed twice a day as part of my daily healing routine.

The Tomatis therapy began to take on an even higher meaning when talking to a client who had actually attended one of these courses. This had led him to explore the "Inner Sound" therapy developed by Arden Wilken in which twelve layers of hertz frequencies reach up to 4082 Hz. As had been the pattern, everybody was ready to be involved with higher frequencies than the Solfeggio tones formerly used, the highest of which was 963 Hz. Of course, the ears would need some preparation to receive higher healing frequencies and this would also probably develop brain potential which should not be a problem since it is well known that human beings only use a small proportion of brain capacity. This was all very interesting.

The next focus was on the chakra system. In his book, *Shaman Healer Sage*, Alberto Villodo gives a very detailed account of the importance of the chakra system which is linked to the spine, the central nervous system and, of course, to the endocrine glands. Villodo reminds us that the Amazon Shamans believe that we develop a *"rainbow body"* when the chakras are all cleared. Another "rainbow" reference!

I had to give much colour healing/cleansing using all the colours of the spectrum and this started with a lot of red colour healing at the root chakra. This is the chakra that houses, amongst other things, past life traumas. Oestrogen and testosterone are the hormones associated with this chakra. When the hormonal situation is unbalanced it can cause big problems, especially for men. They may seek physical satisfaction through sex at the expense of the inner harmony that all human intimacy so desires. Going even further, much sexual abuse could, in fact, be a deeper cry for help. It was interesting to notice that at this time there was much media attention surrounding "cover-up" affairs. As we reach a higher level of understanding, hopefully people will become more aware of deeper causes before judging too superficially.

If I thought the cleansing of the chakra system was just to be another stage that we would pass through fairly quickly, then I was in for a surprise. In fact, I gradually came to understand that nobody had ever had a properly functioning system! This was probably because we had been carrying not only our own past life issues and those of our ancestors, but also all the "collective cosmic memories"! Since December 2009, we had been clearing all the "top layers", thus paving the path for the Heller therapy to "unlock the chest of traumas" housed in the root chakra. In order to release all the accumulated misery, session upon session of lavender colour healing was needed followed by cleansing with Zeolite and Milk Thistle. After all this clearance it wasn't surprising to find everyone needed oxygen, oxygen and oxygen! According to current information, we are discovering the power of oxygen and how it can heal and replace damaged cells and organs, activate the immune system and lead to increased energy... not obvious to my clients yet! However, considering the significant amount of oxygen that was needed, I felt it was probably regenerating all the cells. So, perhaps we were now reaching a level of healing never experienced before!

The subject of the toxicity of dental amalgam fillings had often crossed my mind. I had hoped that with so much ongoing cleansing from powerful sources the toxicity may have been addressed, but, unfortunately, this was not the case. It had become an issue and it was now important to release these undesirable side effects. Since we have become "Cosmic Beings" the body may not tolerate the levels of toxicity associated with outdated dental procedures.

Opticians don't know how the eyes are being affected by all the changes and vets, of course, need to leave old tools behind. They should cease the procedure of putting animals to sleep. I became specifically aware of this when, recently, I had begun to pick up grief stricken animals after "untimely" death.

Information had been reaching me to confirm how very important our healing journey was, since from the beginning of 2013 there were *"incredible shifts in energy, vibration and consciousness affecting everyone's body"*. These were *"to accelerate the transformation from our carbon based planetary bodies into crystalline based Solar Light Beings"*. How exciting!

CHAPTER 32

*...Thus was the Unicorn the first beast that man beheld and
the first to which he gave a name. From that time to this, fates
of these two races have been bound together, for while the
Unicorn leads towards the Light, only man may pass therein...*

The Unicornis Manuscripts by Michael Green

I have always loved the image of the unicorn to which I dedicated a few lines of verse that appear in my first book *From Caterpillar to Butterfly*. It symbolises the purity that is our essence. We shall get a deeper and deeper perception of this as we peel away our dross.

It was now timely to find out about the work of an amazing American woman who, after a lifetime as a dancer, came to realise the great importance of "movement" not only *of*, but also *within* the body. It was during a conversation with a client that I found out about Emilie Conrad. Her organisation in the USA is called "Continuum", and is discussed in her book *Life on Land* published in 2007 (two years before all the physical bodily changes). Emilie Conrad maintains that once the tissue fluid is flowing freely, the body and everything within it can *"renew itself"*. She is convinced of the body's innate capacity to heal itself, as long as we do not interfere with this natural process. She has demonstrated that even people confined to a wheelchair with paralysis due to spinal injury could, in some cases, become mobile again as the spine healed itself. Her work is yet another example that backs up everything I had come to understand myself. However, following my discoveries in December 2009, I believe that the body has to be released from any "irregularities" present at an energetic level *before* the self-healing journey on an inner level can begin.

Discussing the work of Emilie Conrad with another client, she told me how she had come across some similar understanding associated with Moshe Feldenkrais (1904–1984), an Israeli physicist who was born in the Ukraine. He studied in Paris where he later worked in nuclear physics. Coming from a background of Ju-jitsu, he helped to introduce Judo into Europe. In the 1940s, a recurring knee injury started to cause him serious discomfort. Confronted by a medical profession that was unable to help him walk without pain, he realised that he could only count on his own resources. He became aware of the correlation between the mind and the body and started by researching an alternative to a hazardous operation. He gradually developed a new approach to self healing and published *Awareness through Movement* in 1972, in which he lays the bases of a method now known as the Feldenkrais Method.

The ground breaking work of Feldenkrais and Emilie Conrad has influenced other therapies, pushing them towards deeper understanding, as in the case of Cranial Osteopathy and, more recently, Biodynamic Cranial Sacral Therapy.

It was precisely the Biodynamic Cranial Sacral Therapy that I found was needed in the next "collective" healing stage for everybody alongside the ancient Hawaiian massage known as "Kahuna".

This brought us up to July 26th 2013 when another of the "shutdowns" occurred. After a few days, some information came through the post to explain things! The "Lion's Gate" is the name given to the time of year when the sun enters the sign of the Leo. This is also known as the Planetary New Year. During the summer of 2013, the Gate, or "Star Gate", was a period of approximately two weeks when a vortex opened and a wave of intense light from the Galactic Centre was received on Earth. Up to now, because of the low level of awareness on the planet, this energy had been retained in the pyramid complex at Giza. It was now considered to be an appropriate time for Earth to receive the energies through the Earth's Crystalline Grid System in order to recalibrate the planetary frequencies for "Higher Levels of Consciousness". The planet had been in the fifth dimension for ten years, and it was now time for all of us to "catch up"! It was an intense time while the DNA was "upgraded". However, as always, if we trust the process, all will be well.

And "trusting the process" was exactly what I was to be called on to do when, completely out of the blue, one afternoon I got out of my car and noticed discomfort in the groin area. It didn't cause too much of a problem at first, but over the next few weeks, I realised something important was taking place and that it would probably be very significant for everyone else. Nevertheless, in the meantime I now had to fit *myself* in alongside the daily routine of healing work for all of my clients!

I began to need all the healing that suggested major changes taking place in the body. It began with nearly one hour of thought healing with magenta colour healing (for major cellular change) and was followed over the next few weeks by white powder gold (previously talked about), strontium (for bone changes), sound healing, the Flower of Life (geometrical re-patterning), purple colour healing which decreases sensitivity to pain and many sessions of some "new tool" therapies; Muscular Harmoniser Technique, Cranial Osteopathy and the Feldenkrais Therapy recently mentioned. Eventually, strontium was again needed alongside something called Cymatics.

I had known about Cymatics ever since I did my Colour Therapy training. A man called Dr Peter Guy Manners came to give us a talk about his use of Cymatics at the Bretforton Hall Clinic in Worcestershire.

Cymatics is the study of how sound affects matter. In the 18th-century, Ernst Chladni was the first to show how specific sound vibrations form geometric patterns in sand. In the 1960s, Hans Jenny used a modern frequency generator and coined the term "Cymatics" from the Greek word for "wave". Dr. Peter Guy Manners built on the work of his predecessors and developed the therapy of Cymatics based on the idea of transmitting into a diseased area of the body the precise sound frequencies of healthy organs and tissues. He developed a frequency generator called Mark I that progressively became Mark VI. Today, modern Cymatherapy delivers a computerised combination of sound and magnetic therapy applied directly to the body to normalise imbalance and synchronise cell frequencies back into a health state of resonance, thus supporting the body's natural ability to heal itself.

Much like Alfred Tomatis, Dr Peter Guy Manners, who died in 2009, was a precursor in the field of sound therapy. The harmonising of the sound frequencies within the cells of our individual bodies will certainly help to bring us into compatibility with the ongoing changing frequencies of planet Earth.

As soon as I found that I needed Cymatics, it moved everyone else into needing this therapy on a daily basis.

The higher consciousness of the body always "knows" exactly the order in which healing should take place, and so it was important at this point for a client to mention the word "Somatics" from the Greek "Somatikos" which could be translated as "Living, aware bodily person". Somatic therapy is a holistic therapy that integrates our physical, mental, emotional, and spiritual aspects. Taking time to focus on what we are feeling or experiencing helps to repair the body/mind split which is especially prevalent in our western culture.

Somatic therapy through thought was eventually needed by everyone twice a day. Bodily pain can be released when the body is viewed as a tool to be worked *with*, not *on*. This harks back to the understanding of Emilie Conrad and her "Continuum" concept and also to the work of Moshe Feldenkrais. The Somatic therapy was immediately followed by lavender colour healing to remind us yet again of the need to release unhappiness.

On a more anecdotal level this was also the period when I began to notice that many of my thought sessions involved healing for eleven, twenty-two, or thirty-three minutes and very often when I happened to look at my clock, it indicated the minutes of master numbers! It indeed was a reflection of how sacred numerology is involved in every aspect of meaningful life!

I also discovered that I could now pick up the energy fields of everybody in a much quicker time than even a few years ago and my thought healing had reached a stage where any irregularities in the body itself and the brain could now be corrected and healed. This would not have been possible before. I put this down to the new high planetary energy vibration, confirming, yet again, that we are indeed rising to new levels of consciousness.

From the book *Inside an Autistic World* translated from German, and published by Temple Lodge in 2013, it is suggested that the wide spectrum of issues in the field of autism is due to very traumatic past life experiences. As karma has been released from the planet it was timely for so many people with these sorts of problems to suddenly begin to cross my path and for whom I had permission to do corrective healing work.

Just a few days before the end of 2013, a major event started to emerge when everybody suddenly needed three long thought sessions of magenta colour healing (for fine chemical cellular changes). This reminded me of my own experience a few months earlier, and seemed to confirm some of the work of Dr Berrenda Fox. In the early years of 2000, she had described her work on cellular mutation and the massive physical changes that would occur to human beings as we transform into a new "species" while still in our present bodies. I'm sure we shall only understand the full implications of such changes as the months of 2014 unfurl.

Perhaps human beings are indeed getting ready to emerge from the caterpillar cocoon to glimpse a new butterfly perspective of the world! I was reminded of the lovely words made famous by the black American singer, Louis Armstrong and sung at a time that wasn't easy for the black community. *"And I think to myself what a wonderful world"*.

CHAPTER 33

There is nothing beyond love. Everything in life in all
dimensions is leading towards love. Love is the centre of all
being, all knowing and all understanding. Beyond karma sees
the re-birth of love.

The Creator Speaks Michelle Phillips

What a lovely quote as we journey into the New Age. An incredible journey in many ways.

We are uncovering so much of our ancient history through the Pleiadian books and more recently in *The Coming of the Holy Grail* by Claire Nahmad and Michael Revill. They chart some of the lost understanding of the history of the world that lies in the secret crypt in the grounds of Lincoln cathedral! The very detailed research that was carried out by these authors could easily have filled two books! However, it is fascinating to discover how they weave their findings into the Lewis Carroll *Alice's Adventures in Wonderland* story as truth for our time.

Now that planet Earth has been bathed in the highest light energies ever before experienced we can go on renewing ourselves as the Creator intended. Messages to Earth are that our planet is to become the aforementioned Cosmic Library for the rest of the universe to evolve. Latest messages from St Germain are *"get out of your heads into your hearts"* This can allow us to experience the "inner joy", and as our feeling centres open up, we will begin to see others as a reflection of divinity at the heart of all life.

Not by chance, I received information that during October 2013 the Archangel Michael and his Legions of Power would create a forcefield of protection against stress on the subtle bodies of human beings and a new renaissance of divine love would be flowing into every particle and wave of life on Earth. As we all adjust to this, we are informed that it will be *"glorious beyond our wildest imagination"*.

I wanted to end this book on a chapter associated with a Master Number vibration. The symbolism of the number thirtythree is *"compassion leading to love"*. It therefore seems appropriate to quote *"what may be the definitive version"* of the prayer of St Francis as sung (track eleven!) on a lovely recording by a young friar from the Franciscan Order of St Francis of Assisi. It is less well known that St Francis lived in the era of troubadours and often sought to express life through poetry and song. Friar Alessandro, following in this tradition *"seeks to be a channel of joy to the listener"*.

Make me a channel of your peace
Where there is hatred, let me bring your love
Where there is injury, your pardon, Lord
And where there is doubt, true faith in you

Oh Master, grant that I may never seek
So much to be consoled, as to console
To be understood as to understand
To be loved as to love with all my soul

Make me a channel of your peace
Where there is despair in life, let me bring hope
Where there is darkness, only light
And where there is sadness, ever joy

Make me a channel of your peace
It is in pardoning that we are pardoned, Lord
In giving to all men, that we receive
And in dying that we are born to eternal life.